DATA SCIENCE WITH PYTHON

The Ultimate Step-by-Step Guide for Beginners to Learn Python for Data Science

Julian James McKinnon

Table of Contents

INTRODUCTION 9

    Effectiveness of Libraries for Python 11

    There Is Always Someone Available to Help in the Python Community 12

CHAPTER 1: WHAT IS DATA SCIENCE? 14

    The Importance of Data Science 15

    How Is Data Science Used? 19

    The Lifecycle of Data Science 21

    The Components of Data Science 23

CHAPTER 2: BASICS OF PYTHON 26

    Python IDEs 26

        Sublime Text 26

        Atom 27

        Eclipse 27

    Getting Started with Python 27

        Basic Syntax 27

        Identifiers 28

        Variables and Data Types 29

    Data Types 29

        Decision Making and Basic Operators 30

    Functions and Modules 32

    Object-Oriented Programming 33

Class Inheritance 35

Regular Expressions 36

Match and Search Functions 38

Exception Handling 38

File Handling 40
  Opening a File *40*
  Closing a File *41*
  Writing into Existing Files *41*
  Deleting Files *41*
  Deleting a Folder *42*

CHAPTER 3: THE BEST PYTHON LIBRARIES FOR DATA SCIENCE 43

Core Libraries and Statistics 44
  NumPy *44*
  SciPy *46*
  Pandas *47*
  Matplotlib *48*
  Scikit-Learn *50*
  Theano *51*
  TensorFlow *52*
  Keras *54*

Visualization 56

Machine Learning Libraries 58

Deep Learning 59

CHAPTER 4: DATA SCIENCE AND APPLICATIONS ... 62

Banking and Finance 63
  Fraud Detection 64
  Customer Data Management 65
  Investment Banks Risk Modeling 66
  Personalized Marketing 67
Health and Medicine 67
  Analysis of Medical Image 68
  Genomics and Genetics 68
  Drugs Creation 69
  Virtual Assistance for Customer and Patients Support ... 70
  Industry Knowledge 71
Oil and Gas 71
  Immediate Drag Calculation and Torque Using Neural Networks 72
  Predicting Well Production Profile Through Feature Extraction Models 73
  Downstream Optimization 73
The Internet 74
  Targeted Advertising 74
  Website Recommendations 75
  Advanced Image Recognition 76
  Speech Recognition 76
Travel and Tourism 76
  Customer Segmentation and Personalized Marketing 77
  Analysis of Customer Sentiment 78
  Recommendation Engine 79
  Travel Support Bots 79
  Route Optimization 80

CHAPTER 5: THE LIFECYCLE OF DATA SCIENCE 82

The Discovery Phase 83

The Data Preparation Phase 84

The Model Planning Phase 87

The Operationalize Phase 91

The Communicate Results Phase 93

CHAPTER 6: PROBABILITY, STATISTICS, AND DATA TYPES 95

Real-Life Probability Examples 95

Organize Around the Weather 96

Strategies in Sports 96

Insurance Option 97

Recreational and Games Activities 98

Statistics 99

Statistics in Data Analysis 100

Data Types 104

Categorical Data 104

Nominal Data 105

Ordinal Data 105

Numerical Data 106

The Importance of Data Types 107

Statistical Methods 108

Nominal Data 108

Ordinal Data 109

Continuous Data 109

Descriptive Statistics 110
Normal Distribution *110*
Central Tendency *111*

CHAPTER 7: MOST COMMON DATA SCIENCE PROBLEMS 114

Management Expects the World 115

Misunderstanding How Data Works 118

Taking the Blame for Bad News 120

Communication as a Solution 125

CHAPTER 8: COMPARISON OF PYTHON WITH OTHER LANGUAGES 126

Python versus Java comparison 126

Python versus C# 128

Python versus JavaScript 130

Python versus Perl 131

Python versus Tcl 132

Python versus Smalltalk 132

Python versus C++ 133

Python versus Common Lisp and Scheme 135

Python versus Node.js 138
Favorable Circumstances of Python over Node.js *138*
Lower Section Point *139*
More Applications *139*

Less Obstinate Ecosystem 140

Coding Everything in JavaScript 140
    Quick Development and a Huge Network 140
    Advancement History of Python and JavaScript 141
    Inclining Advances 141
    Execution and Speed 142

Python versus PHP 143
    Python versus PHP for Web Improvement Correlation . 143
    Frameworks 144

CHAPTER 9: DATA CLEANING AND PREPARATION 145

What Is Data Preparation? 146

Why Do I Need Data Preparation? 148

What Are the Steps for Data Preparation? 150

Handling the Missing Data 153

CHAPTER 10: DATA VISUALIZATION 156

Data Visualization to the End-User 156

Matplotlib 160
    Line Chart 161
    Histogram 161
    Bar Chart 161

Visualization Using Pandas 162

The Objective of Visualization 162

The Simplest Method to Complex Visualization of Data 164

Overview of Plotly 165
   Building Attractive Plots Using Plotly *166*
   Scatter Plots *166*
   Box Plots...*167*

Heat Maps..168

CONCLUSION..**171**

© Copyright 2020 by Julian James McKinnon
All rights reserved.

The material contained herein is presented with the intent of furnishing pertinent and relevant information and knowledge on the topic with the sole purpose of providing entertainment. The author should thus not be considered an expert on the topic in this material despite any claims to such expertise, first-hand knowledge, and any other reasonable claim to specific knowledge on the material contained herein.

The information presented in this work has been researched to ensure its reasonable accuracy and validity.

Nevertheless, it is advisable to consult with a duly licensed professional in the area pertaining to this topic, or any other covered in this book, in order to ensure the quality and validity of the advice and/or techniques contained in this material.

This is a legally binding statement as deemed so by the Committee of Publishers Association and the American Bar Association in the United States.

Any reproduction, transmission, copying, or otherwise duplication of the material contained in this work are in violation of current copyright legislation.

No physical or digital copies of this work, both total and partial, may not be done without the Publisher's express written consent. All additional rights are reserved by the publisher of this work.

The data, facts, and description of events forthwith shall be considered as accurate unless the work is deemed to be a work of fiction.

In any event, the Publisher is exempt of responsibility for any use of the information contained in the present work on the part of the user.

The author and publisher may not be deemed liable, under any circumstances, for the events resulting from the observance of the advice, tips, techniques and any other contents presented herein.

Given the informational and entertainment nature of the content presented in this work, there is no guarantee as to the quality and validity of the information.

As such, the contents of this work are deemed as universal.

No use of copyrighted material is used in this work.

Any references to other trademarks are done so under fair use and by no means represent an endorsement of such trademarks or their holder.

Introduction

Python is termed as a multi-paradigm language used for programming and can be perceived as a Swiss army knife in the field of coding.

It can support OOP, functional programming patterns, and structured programming, among several other things.

There is a saying popularly used in the community of Python, and it goes like this: Python is normally the 2nd best language for all purposes.

But this isn't a knock for organizations faced with the dilemma of using the best of the breed solutions as they soon find themselves burdened with codebases that are unmaintainable and incompatible.

Python is capable of handling all the jobs from data mining to website building to the running of embedded systems.

It is an all-in-one programming language.

For instance, in the case of ForecastWatch, Python was utilized for writing a parser for harvesting forecasts from other sites.

It is also used for an aggregate engine that compiles the data and the website code for displaying results.

It was PHP, which was originally utilized for building the website until the organization realized that it was a lot easier to deal with a single language for everything.

Facebook also selected Python for data analysis because it was being used a great deal for other portions of the organization.

The name Python is derived from the popular rock band Monty Python.

The creator of the Python programming language, Guido Van Possum, chose this name to suggest that its use would be fun.

You will find many obscure Monty Python sketches, which are referenced in the code samples used in Python and those used for documentation.

For these reasons, this is a cherished programming language among programmers.

The data scientists with scientific or engineering backgrounds might feel like a barber armed with an ax when they use the language for the first time for data analysis—out of place.

However, the inherent simplicity and readability of Python make it comparatively easy to pick, and the quantity of devoted analytical libraries available nowadays mean that data scientists in all sectors can find packages tailored for their needs, easily available on the net for downloads.

Due to the general nature of Python and its extensibility, it was inevitable that as the popularity of the language went into an orbit, its use in the field of data science became a foregone conclusion.

As a matter of fact, Python is a—jack of all trades—program, and it isn't particularly well-suited for statistical analysis.

However, several companies have invested in Python, realizing the advantages of using a standardized language and extending it for those purposes.

Effectiveness of Libraries for Python

Similar to other programming languages, the main reason for the success of Python is the libraries.

There are around 72,000 of them available with the PyPi (Python Package Index), and the number is constantly rising.

Python is specifically designed to possess a stripped-down and lightweight core, and its standard library is built by using tools that can be utilized in all programming tasks.

Python comes with a "batteries included" philosophy that allows its users to get down to the issue of finding solutions to problems quickly without having to go across many competing function libraries.

There Is Always Someone Available to Help in the Python Community

There are many great things about Python, and one of them is the broad and diverse base of millions of Python users all across the globe who are ready to offer suggestions and advice when you're stuck on something.

There is a very good chance that someone else was stuck on the same problem before you.

These open source communities are extremely popular due to their open discussion attitude.

However, some of them are pretty fierce about not allowing newcomers to mix easily.

Python is, happily, an exception.

These Python experts are happy to aid you, both online and during the local meet-ups.

Chances are, you will stumble into several intricacies of learning a new programming language.

As Python plays such a vital role in the data science community, you can find several resources that are specific to the use of Python in the data sciences.

These meet-up groups of data scientists who use Python are prevalent all across the US, especially in places such as Los Angeles and Seattle.

In case you're having trouble locating a meet-up group near you that has the right qualifications, there is a data science hack that uses Python for searching these meet-up groups to find the perfect match.

Chapter 1: What Is Data Science?

The first thing that we need to take some time looking over in this guidebook is the basics of data science.

Data science, to keep things simple, is the detailed study of the flow of information from the huge amounts of data that a company has gathered and stored.

It is going to involve obtaining some meaningful insights out of raw and usually unstructured data that can then be processed through analytical programming and business skills.

Many companies are going to spend a lot of time collecting data and trying to use it to learn more about their customers, figure out how to release the best product, and learning how to gain a competitive edge over others.

While these are all great goals, just gathering the data is not going to be enough to make it happen.

Instead, we need to be able to take that data, and that data is usually pretty messy and needs some work and analyze it so that we are better able to handle all that comes with it.

The Importance of Data Science

In a world that is going more and more to the digital space, organizations are going to deal with unheard of amounts of data, but structured and unstructured, on a daily basis.

Evolving technologies are going to enable some cost savings for us, and smarter storage spaces to help us store some of this critical data.

Currently, no matter what kind of industry we are looking at or what kind of work the company does, there is already a huge need for skilled and knowledgeable data scientists.

They are actually some of the highest-paid IT professionals right now, mainly because they can provide such a good value for the companies they work for, and because there is such a shortage of these professionals.

The gap of data scientists versus the current supply is about 50 percent, and it is likely to continue growing as more people and companies start to see what value data science can have for them.

So, why is data becoming so important to these businesses?

In reality, data has always been important, but today, because of the growth in the internet and other sources, there is an unprecedented amount of data to work through.

In the past, companies were able to manually go through the data they had, and maybe use a few business intelligence tools to learn more about the customer and to make smart decisions.

But this is nearly impossible for any company to do now thanks to the large amount of data they have to deal with on a regular basis.

In the last few years, there has been a huge amount of growth in something known as the "Internet of Things", due to which about 90 percent of the data has been generated in our current world.

This sounds even more impressive when we find out that each day, 2.5 quintillion bytes of data are generated and used, and it is more accelerated with the growth of the IoT.

This data is going to come to us from a lot of different sources, and where you decide to gather this data is going to depend on your goals and what you are hoping to accomplish in the process.

Some of the places where we are able to gather this kind of data will include:

- Sensors are used in malls and other shopping locations in order to gather more information about the people who shop there.
- Posts placed on various social media sites.
- Digital videos and pictures are captured on our phones.

- Purchase transactions that are made through e-commerce.

These are just a few places where we are able to gather up some of the data that we need and put it to use with data science.

And as the IoT grows and more data is created on a daily basis, it is likely that we are going to find even more sources that will help us to take on our biggest business problems.

And this leads us to need data science more than ever.

All of this data that we are gathering from the sources above and more will be known as big data.

Currently, most companies are going to be flooded and a bit overwhelmed by all of the data that is coming their way.

This is why it is so important for these companies to have a good idea of what to do with the exploding amount of data and how they are able to utilize it to get ahead.

It is not enough to just gather up the data.

This may seem like a great idea, but if you just gather up that data, and don't learn what is inside of it, then you are leading yourself to trouble.

Once you can learn what information is inside of that data, and what it all means, you will find that it is much easier to use that information to give yourself the competitive advantage that you are looking for.

Data science is going to help us to get all of this done.

It is designed to make it easier for us to really take in the big picture and use data for our needs.

It will encompass all of the parts of the process of getting the data to work for us, from gathering the data to cleaning it up and organizing it, to analyzing it, to creating visuals to help us better understand the data, and even to the point of how we decide to use that data.

All of this comes together and helps us to really see what is inside of the data, and it is all a part of the data science process.

Data science is going to work because it is able to bring together a ton of different skills, like statistics, mathematics, and business domain knowledge, and can help out a company in many ways.

Some of the things that data science is able to do when it is used in the proper manner for a company, will include some of the following:

- Reduce costs.
- Get the company into a new market.
- Tap into a new demographic to increase their reach.
- Gauge the effectiveness of a marketing campaign.
- Launch a new service or a new product.

And this is just the start of the list.

If you are willing to work with data science and learn the different steps that come with it, you will find that it is able to help your business out in many different manners, and it can be one of the best options for you to use in order to get ahead in your industry.

How Is Data Science Used?

One of the best ways to learn more about data science and how it works is to take a look at how some of the top players in the industry are already using data science.

There are a ton of big-name companies who are already relying on data science to help them reach their customers better, keep waste and costs down, and so much more.

For example, some of the names that we are going to take a look at here include Google, Amazon, and Visa.

As you will see with all of these, one of the biggest deciding factors for an organization is what value they think is the most important to extract from their data using analytics, and how they would like to present that information as well.

Let's take a look at how each of these companies has been able to use data science for their needs to see some results.

First on the list is Google.

This is one of the biggest companies right now that is on a hiring spree for trained data scientists.

Google has been driven by data science in a lot of the work that they do, and they also rely on machine learning and artificial intelligence in order to reach their customers and to ensure that they are providing some of the best products possible to customers as well.

Data science and some good analysis have been able to help them get all of this done effectively.

Next on the list is the company Amazon.

This is a huge company known around the world, one that many of us use on a daily basis.

It is a cloud computing and e-commerce site that relies heavily on data scientists to help them release new products, keep customer information safe, and even to do things like providing recommendations on what to purchase next on the site.

They will use the data scientist to help them find out more about the mindset of the customer and to enhance the geographical reach of their cloud domain and their e-commerce, just to name a few of their business goals right now.

And then, we need to take a look at the Visa company and what they are doing with the help of data science.

As an online financial gateway for countless other companies, Visa ends up completing transactions that are worth hundreds of millions in one day, much more than what other companies can even dream about.

Due to the large number of transactions that are going on, Visa needs data scientists to help them increase their revenue, check if there are any fraudulent transactions, and even to customize some products and services based on the requirements of the customer.

The Lifecycle of Data Science

We are going to go into more detail about the lifecycle of data science as we progress through this guidebook, but first, we can take a moment just to see how we are able to use this for our own needs.

Data science is going to follow our data from the gathering stage of the data, all the way through until we use that data to make our big business decisions.

There are a number of steps that are going to show up in the process in the meantime, and being prepared to handle all of these, and all that they entail, is the challenge that comes when we want to rely on data science.

Some of the basic steps that are found in the data science lifecycle are going to include:

- Figuring out what business question we would like to answer with this process.

- The process of collecting raw data for use.

- Cleaning and organizing all unstructured data to be used.

- Preprocessing our data.

- Creating a model with the help of machine learning and taking some time to train and test it to ensure accurate results along the way.

- Running our data through the model to help us understand what insights and predictions are inside.

- Use visuals to help us better understand the complex relationships that are found in any data that we are using for this analysis.

While the steps may sound easy enough to work with, there are going to be some complexities and a lot of back and forth that we have to work with here.

The most important thing here is to go into it without any preconceived notions of what you would like to see happening and don't try to push your own agenda on the data.

This is the best way to ensure that you will actually learn what is inside of that data and can make it easier to choose the right decisions for your needs as well.

The Components of Data Science

Now, we also need to take some time to look at the basics of data science.

There are going to be a few key components that come into play when we are talking about data science, and having these in place is going to make a big difference in how well we are able to handle some of the different parts that come with data science, and how we can take on some of the different parts that we need with our own projects.

Some of the key components that we need to take a look at when it comes to data science will include:

- **The Various Types of Data:** The foundation of any data science project is going to be the raw set of data. There are a lot of different types. We can work with the structured data that is mostly found in tabular form, and the unstructured data, which is going to include PDF files, emails, videos, and images.

- **Programming:** You will need some kind of programming language to get the work done, with Python and R being the best option. Data management and data analysis are going to be done with some computer programming. Python and R are the two most popular programming languages that we will focus on here.

- **Statistics and Probability:** Data is going to be manipulated in different ways in order to extract some good information out of it. The mathematical foundation of data science is going to be probability and statistics. Without having a good knowledge of probability and statistics, there is going to be a higher possibility of misinterpreting the data and reaching conclusions that are not correct. This is a big reason why the probability and statistics that we are looking at here are going to be so important in data science.

- **Machine Learning:** As someone who is working with data science, you are going to spend at least a little time learning the algorithms of machine learning on a daily basis. This can include methods of classification and regression. It is important for a data scientist to know machine learning to complete their job, since this is the tool that is needed to help predict valuable insights from the data that is available.

- **Big Data:** In our current world, raw data is going to be what we use to train and test our models and then figure out the best insights and predictions out of that data. Working with big data is going to help us to figure out what important, although hidden, information is found in our raw data. There are a lot of different tools that we are able to use in order to help us not only find the big data but also to process some of these big data as well.

There are many companies that are learning the value of data science and all that is going to come with it.

They like the idea that they can take all of the data they have been collecting for a long period of time and put it to use to increase their business and give them that competitive edge they have been looking for.

In the rest of this guidebook, we are going to spend some time focusing on how to work with data science and all of the different parts that come with it as well.

Chapter 2: Basics of Python

Python IDEs

An Integrated Development Environment is a tool that provides facilities like build automation, testing, code lining, and debugging for different programming languages.

Python IDEs are best suited for developing machine learning and deep analytics models.

Here are some of the best IDEs for Python programming:

Sublime Text

Sublime Text is an amazing code editor that provides high customizability and is best for beginners.

Along with other popular programming languages, Sublime Text also supports Python execution and comes with predefined support for the language.

The editor can be downloaded free of cost and is considered a full-fledged Python development environment.

Sublime Text packages are written in Python programming language, which provides a wide range of extensions and packages to support complex programming.

Atom

Atom is an open-source integrated development environment designed and developed by Github.

Users can download and install the IDE along with predefined development packages such as linter-flake8 and python-debugger.

Being highly customizable, users can install packages and set up the environment to meet their development requirements.

Eclipse

Eclipse is an all-rounder integrated development environment that is available for Windows, Linux, and OS X.

The tool has a rich marketplace of add-ons and extensions, which makes it suitable for machine learning and Python development.

Furthermore, the PyDev extension allows the developers to perform Python debugging and utilize code completion facilities as well.

Getting Started with Python

Basic Syntax

For writing your first Python program, you are required to be well aware of the basic syntax and requirements of the Python programming language.

A Python program can be written and executed in two basic modes, which are known as Interactive mode and Script mode.

In the Interactive mode, developers are supposed to write a program and execute it, whereas, in the Script mode, files and code can be saved and accessed through the Python program (.py file).

Identifiers

Identifiers are used to identify a module, class, function, or variable in a program.

In the Python programming language, an identifier can be a letter from A to Z or from a to z followed by zero or more digits, underscores, or letters.

Furthermore, the Python language does not allow characters such as %, $, or @ within identifiers.

Being a case-sensitive language, programmers need to place identifiers carefully to execute the program without any error.

Python syntax can be executed by writing the following line in the command line:

\>> print("Hello world!")

Hello world

Variables and Data Types

Similar to other major programming languages such as Java, C, and C++, Python has predefined data types and rules for using variables.

For Python programming, you must remember that a variable can have both short and descriptive variables like x, y, age, or year.

A variable name should always start with a letter and cannot start with a number.

Moreover, variable names are case-sensitive in Python, and developers need to be careful when declaring variables in the program.

Data Types

Python has built-in default data types, which include text, numeric, sequence, mapping, Set and Boolean and Binary type.

To get the data type in the Python programming language, the "type()" function can be used in the program.

Here are some examples of setting data types in Python:

Sample	Data Type
x = " Python"	Str

x = 5	Int
x = 5.0	float
x = range (5)	range
x = ("Red", "Blue")	Tuple
x = ["Red", "Blue"]	list
x = True/False	Boolean
x = b "Python"	bytes

Decision Making and Basic Operators

Decision-making is an essential part of any programming language because it specifies the program to take actions according to the given conditions.

If statement

Syntax:

if expression:

statement

If-else statement

Syntax:

if expression:

>statement

else:

>statement

Nested If statements

In a nested, if statement, we can have an if, elif, and else present within another if, elif, and else statement.

The syntax for implementing this statement is defined as follows:

If first_expression:

>Write your statement here

>if second_expression:

>write your statement here

>elif third_expression:

>write your statements here

>else:

>write the default statement

Functions and Modules

Python has built-in functions that can be used to create a number of complex machine learning and deep learning models.

Built-in functions are also known as user-defined functions.

For defining a function in the Python programming language, we can use the syntax as described below:

Def function name(parameters) :

"function docstring"

 function suite

 return [expression]

For example:

Def printme (str):

    "Sample string passed into a function"

    print str

    return

Modules in Python programming allow developers to organize their code and develop code modules that can be used further in the program.

A module is also referred to as a file made up of Python code, which includes arbitrarily named attributes, classes, variables, and functions.

For example:

def print func(parameter):

    print "Sample:", parameter

    return

Furthermore, we can also import an existing module into the Python source code by using the import module support.

Here are some of the import statement modules for the Python programming language:

- import statement
- from.. import statement: from modname import*

Object-Oriented Programming

Python is based on object-oriented programming modules that enable developers to perform different tasks through classes and objects.

In OOP, a class is a user-defined prototype that is defined for an object and contains a set of attributes, data members, class variables, and instance variables.

A class variable is shared with each instance of the class and is usually defined outside the class method.

Furthermore, class variables cannot be used more often as compared to instance variables.

An instance variable is defined inside a method and only belongs to the current instance of a class.

In object-oriented programming, the function overloading approach is referred to as the implementation of more than one behavior to a specific function.

To implement classes in a program, we are required to make use of objects and methods in the class definition.

Here is the syntax to create a class in Python:

Class ClassName:

    "class documentation string"

    Class_suite

Sample pupil class in Python:

class Pupil:

  'Base class for Students"

  empCount = 0

  def __init__(self, fname, Marks):

self.name = fname

self.marks = marks

Pupil.pupCount += 1

  def displayCount(self):

print "Total Number of Pupils%d" % Pupil.pupCount

  def displayPupil(self):

  print "Name : ", self.name, ", Marks: ", self.marks

To access class attributes, we can use the following syntax:

pup.1displayPupil()

pup.2displayPupil()

print "Pupil %d" % Pupil.pupCount

In a Python class, there are several built-in attributes that can be accessed by using the dot operator.

For example, dict, doc, name, module, and bases.

Class Inheritance

In object-oriented programming, a class can be created by deriving it from an existing class.

The child class inherits the attributes from its parent class, and they can also be used to override data members, functions, and methods from the parent class.

Furthermore, the derived classes are the same in functionality as their parent class.

For example:

class A: // Class A definition

..

class B: // Class B definition

..

class C(A, B): //Subclass A and B

Python syntax:

class SubClassName (ParentClass1[, ParentClass2, ..]):

    "class documentation string"

    Class_suite

Regular Expressions

Regular expression or RegEx is referred to as the sequence of characters that is implemented to create a search pattern.

For developing machine learning and data analytics models, regular expressions are widely used for pattern matching and training of models.

Python comes with a built-in regular expression module, which is also known as re module or RegEx module.

To import the module, we can use the "import re" statement in the program.

The re module is comprised of different functions that can be used to search a string for a match.

For example, search, split, sub, and findall are the major functions that are used for pattern matching and learning in machine learning models.

Implementation:

findall () function

import re

str = "Machine learning"

x = re.findall("in", str)

print(x)

Search() function

import re

str = "Machine learning"

x = re.search("\s", str)

print("Position of first white-space character:", x.start())

Split () function

import re

str = "Machine learning"

x = re.split("\s", str)

print(x)

Match and Search Functions

The match function has the capability to match the re-pattern to the string.

The syntax for match function is defined as follows:

re.match(pattern, string, flags=0)

In the search function, the first occurrence of re-pattern is searched within optional flags and the string.

The syntax for search function is defined as follows:

re.search(pattern, string, flags=0)

Furthermore, regular expression literals can also include an optional modifier.

The optional modifier has the capability to control different aspects of matching, and they are also considered as an optional flag.

Exception Handling

An exception occurs during program execution and can disrupt the smooth flow of program instructions.

When an exception occurs in a Python program, it can be handled through 'try' and 'except' statements as explained below:

try:

  statements

except Exception 1:

  //if exception 1 occurred, execute this block

exception 2:

  //if exception 2 occurred, execute this block

else

No exception occurred

There are different exceptions and assertions which can occur in a Python program.

For example: Exception, StopIteration, SystemExit, StandardError, OverflowError, ArithmeticError, ZeroDivisionError, AssertionError, ImportError, KeyboardInterrupt, LookupError, IndexError, KeyError, and NameError.

It must be noted that a single try statement can have various except statements, and they are only used when the try block has statements that might throw any type of exception.

Furthermore, the Python program might also execute a generic except clause and handle any type of exception.

File Handling

File handling is an essential part of every web or desktop application.

The approach is used to create, read, update, and delete files from the database of the program.

In Python programming, file handling is generally performed with the open() function and includes filename and mode parameters.

Opening a File

To open a file through a Python program, we can use four different modes defined as follows:

Read: Opens a file for reading and initiates an error in case the file does not exist.

Write: Opens file for writing and automatically creates a file if it is not available.

Append: Opens file for appending and creates if not available.

Create: Creates the required file and initiates an error if the file already exists.

The basic syntax for file handling operations:

To open a file: f = open("samplefile.txt"o

To open a file on server:

f = open("samplefile.txt", "r")

print(f.read())

Closing a File

f = open("Filename.txt","r")

print(f.readline())

f.close

Writing into Existing Files

f = open("samplefile.txt", "a")

f.write("New content")

f.close()

f = open("samplefile.txt", "r")

print(f.read())

Create new file: f = open("Newfile.txt", "x")

Deleting Files

To remove or delete a file in Python, you are required to import an OS module for which the os.remove() function is recommended.

The syntax for deleting or removing a file in the Python programming language is defined as follows:

import os

os.remove("Samplefile.txt")

Deleting a Folder

To delete a specific folder, we can use the following syntax:

import os

os.rmdir("Folder")

Chapter 3: The Best Python Libraries for Data Science

Before we dive into seeing some of the cool things that we are able to do when it comes to working with data science and machine learning with Python, we first need to explore some of the different libraries that we need to focus on to make all of this work.

We have to remember with this one that while there are a lot of neat things that we are able to do with the help of the Python language, there are also going to be a few places where it falls behind and may not work as well as we would like.

And this is why we are able to add in some of the best Python libraries and extensions that are designed to work well with data science and the different steps it requires as well.

Python continues to take on some of the leading positions when it comes to solving tasks of data science and some of the challenges that come with it.

And when we are able to add in some of the libraries that we are going to talk about here, you will find that you are really able to handle all of the different processes that are needed for data science in no time.

Let's take a look at these libraries and what we are able to do with them to help us see some amazing results.

Core Libraries and Statistics

NumPy

When we first get started with doing some data science on Python, one of the best libraries to download is going to be NumPy.

This is going to be the best library to work with when it is time to process some large multi-dimensional arrays and matrices.

It also has a pretty extensive collection of mathematical functions and implements methods that will make it possible for us to perform various operations with all of these objects.

Many of the other data science libraries are going to rely on some of the capabilities that come with this kind of library, so having it set up and ready to go on your computer is going to make a big difference.

Over the past few years, there have been a number of improvements that have been made to the library.

In addition to fixing the bugs and dealing with some of the compatibility issues, some of the crucial changes that we are going to see are the possibilities of styling, namely the printing format that comes with the objects in NumPy.

There is also the ability of some functions to handle files of any encoding that you can traditionally do with Python.

When you are ready to start working with some of the scientific tasks with Python, you are going to need to work with the Python SciPy Stack.

This is going to be a collection of software that is specifically designed to help us complete some of the scientific computing that we need to do with Python.

Keep in mind that this SciPy stack is not going to be the same thing as the SciPy library, though, so keep the two of these apart.

The stack is going to be pretty big because there are more than 12 libraries that are found inside of it, and we want to put a focal point on the core package, particularly the most essential ones that help with data science.

The most fundamental package around which this computation stack is going to be built around is NumPy, which is going to stand for Numerical Python.

It is going to provide us with an abundance of useful features for operations that you want to handle with matrices and n-arrays.

This library is going to help us with a lot of different tasks that we want to do, including the vectorization of mathematical operations on the NumPy array type, which is going to ameliorate the performance and will speed up the execution that we see at the same time.

SciPy

Another library that we are able to take a look at when it comes to working with the Python language is going to be SciPy.

This is going to be a library of software that we can use to help us handle some of the tasks that we need for engineering and science.

If this is something that your project is going to need to spend some time on, then SciPy is the best library to get it done.

You will quickly find that this library is going to contain some of the different modules that we need in order to help out with optimization, integration, statistics, and even some linear algebra if we would like to name a few of the different tasks that work well with this.

The main thing that we will use with this library and some of the functionality that you will need when bringing it up is that it is something we can build up with the help of the NumPy library from before.

This means that the arrays that we want to use in SciPy are provided to us thanks to the NumPy library.

This library is going to provide us with some of the most efficient numerical routines, as well as some of the numerical integrations that we need, the help of optimization, and a lot of the other options that we need with our specific submodules.

Pandas

We can't go far in our discussion over the libraries in Python that work with data analysis without spending some time looking at the Pandas library.

This one is going to be designed to help us out with all of the different steps that we need with data science, such as collecting the data, sorting it and cleaning it off, and processing the various data points that we are working with as well.

We are even able to take it a bit further and look at some of the visualizations that are needed to help showcase the data in a manner that is easier to work with.

The Pandas library is going to be a package that will come with Python and has been designed so that it can specifically make some of the work that we need with labeled and relational data simple and more intuitive.

Pandas are going to be the best tool that we can use to help out with many of the processes that we want to handle, and this can include some of the data wranglings that need to happen in this process.

In addition to some of the benefits that we have talked about before, the Pandas library is going to work well when it comes to easy and quick data visualization, manipulation, and aggregation, along with some of the other tasks that we need to work with in order to help us get our work done in data science.

Matplotlib

As we are working through some of the libraries and projects that we want to focus on with data science, we are going to find that working with some data visuals can be helpful as well.

These visuals are going to make it easier for us to handle the complex relationships that are found in our information and our data in the first place.

For most people, it is a lot easier to go through and understand the information that we have when it comes to some sort of visual, whether this is in a picture, a graph or chart, or some other method.

At least compared to some of the methods that we can use with reports and spreadsheets.

This is why the visualization process of data is so important when it is time to work with data science.

And this is why we need to look at Matplotlib to help us to take care of these visuals.

Matplotlib is going to be one of the best data science and Python libraries to work with to make sure that we can create and handle some of the simple and most powerful visuals in no time.

It is going to be a really strong piece of software that will help us to take the results that we are getting when we do the algorithms, and then effortlessly turning them into something that we are able to see and understand easier than before.

We have to remember here that when we are working with Matplotlib, you will find that it is going to be low-level.

This means that you are going to need to spend more time writing out more code to help all of this get done and to give us some of the higher-levels of visuals that we would like.

It requires a bit more effort than we are maybe used to working with, but it is going to still provide us with some of the things that we need to get our work done.

Just be aware that it does require some more work.

When we are working with this kind of library, we have to look at it to help us see how we are able to handle pretty much any kind of visual that we would like.

But we have to remember that we are working with a lot of data and go through the algorithms to understand that information first.

Some of the different options that you are able to work with when it comes to these visuals will include the following:

- The step plot

- Contour plots
- Quiver plots
- Spectrograms
- Pie charts
- Histograms
- Bar charts
- Scatter plots
- Line plots

In addition to helping you to work through some of the different plots and graphs that we have above, it is possible to work with a few of the other capabilities that happen with this language and this library.

You can use this kind of library, and some of the features that we need, in order to work with creating grids, legends, and labels to make the formatting of our visuals easier to handle.

There is a lot that we are going to enjoy when it is time to handle these visuals with Matplotlib, and it is definitely an option that you will want to spend some of your time on.

Scikit-Learn

This is going to be an additional package that you are able to get along with the SciPy Stack that we talked about earlier on.

This one was designed to help us out with a few specific functions, like image processing and the facilitation of machine learning.

When it comes to the latter of the two, one of the most prominent is going to be this library compared to all of the others.

It is also one that is built on SciPy and will make a lot of use on a regular basis of the math operations that come with SciPy as well.

This package is a good one to work with because it can expose a concise and consistent interface that programmers are able to use when it is time to work with the ones that go with the most common algorithms of machine learning.

This is going to make it simple to bring machine learning into the production system.

The library is able to combine together quality code and good documentation, which can bring together high performance and ease of use, and it is one of the industry standards when it comes to doing anything that you need with machine learning in Python.

Theano

We can also spend some time working with the Theano library, and we will find how this one is going to work the best when we want to handle more of the deep learning process rather than machine learning like the other options.

This library is going to be a kind of package from Python that is able to handle arrays that are more multi-dimensional, similar to what we saw with the NumPy library and some of the mathematical expressions and operations.

When we work with the Theano library, and we get it all compiled, which means that we get it to run as efficiently as possible on all of the architectures along the way, it is going to help us to get so much done in no time at all.

This library is going to be so great with some of the deep learning that we want to accomplish, and it is worth our time if we want to focus more on the deep learning that we need.

One of the most important things that we will be able to focus on when it comes to working with the Theano library is that it is really great at integrating tightly with the NumPy library on some of the operations that are considered lower in level.

The library is going to help us to optimize any of the GPU and CPU that you are working with, which is going to help us to go through these computations faster than before.

Add in that this library is going to be more efficient and table, and you will get precision in your results that weren't possible in the past, and you will see why this is a great option to go with.

TensorFlow

The next library on the list that we are able to talk about is going to be known as the TensorFlow library.

This is going to be a library that is special because it was originally developed by Google, and it is also going to be open-sourced so that we are able to use it for our own needs in no time.

It also comes with computations for data flow graphs and more that have been sharpened in order to make sure that we can handle machine learning.

In addition, we are going to find that this library is going to be one of the best to choose when it is time to work with neural networks.

These networks are a great type of algorithm to handle because they will help us to handle our data and make some good decisions through the system.

However, we have to remember that this is not something that is only specific to Google's company.

It is going to have enough power behind it and will be general-purpose enough to help us out with some applications that are better for the real world.

One of the biggest features that we are going to need to focus on when it comes to this kind of library is that we are likely to see a lot of nodes that are in many layers when we work with the system.

This is going to be great to work with because it will help us to train any of the artificial neural networks that we have, even when we have a set of data that is really large.

This is going to make it easier to handle some of the models and algorithms that we are looking to create.

For example, this is a library that can help with voice recognition and even the identification of objects in a picture that is presented.

And these are just a few of the options that we will be able to see with this kind of library.

Keras

And the final library that we are going to take a look at in this guidebook is the Keras library.

This is going to be a great open-sourced library that is going to help again with some of the neural networks that we want to handle in this language, especially the ones that happen at a higher level, and it is also written in Python to make things easier.

We will find that when it comes to the Keras library, the whole thing is pretty easy to work with and minimalistic, with some high-level extensibility to help us out.

It is going to use the TensorFlow or Theano libraries as the back end, but right now, Microsoft is working to integrate it with CNTK as a new back end to give us some more options.

Many users are going to enjoy some of the minimalistic design that comes with Keras.

In fact, this kind of design is aimed at making our experimentation as easy and fast as well, because the systems that you will use will still stay compact.

In addition, we will find that Keras is going to be an easy language to get started with, and it can make some of the prototyping that we want to handle easier.

We will also find that the Keras library is going to be written out in pure Python, and it is going to be a higher level just by nature, helping us to get more programming and machine learning done on our own. It is also highly extendable and modular.

Despite the ease of using this library, the simplicity that comes with it, and the high-level orientation, Keras is still going to have enough power to help us get a lot of serious modeling.

The general idea that is going to come with Keras is based on lots of layers, and then everything else that you need for that model is going to be built around all of the layers.

The data is going to be prepared in tensors.

The first layer that comes with this is then responsible for the input of those tensors.

Then the last layer, however many layers this may be down the road, is going to be responsible for the output.

We will find that all of the other parts of the model are going to be built in between on this to help us get the results that we would like.

And finally, we need to work with StatsModels.

This is going to be one of the modules that come with Python, and it is going to provide us with some chances to work with statistical data analysis.

This includes things like a model estimation and helping us to perform some statistical tests when they are needed.

With the help of this library, we are going to be able to implement a lot of the methods of machine learning that we want, while exploring some of the different possibilities when it comes to plotting.

Visualization

One thing that we need to focus on when it comes to working with machine learning and data science is figuring out how to take some of the insights and patterns that we find, and turning them into a visual that we are able to handle as well.

You will need to work with a specific library to help make sure that you are able to get these visuals taken care of overall.

The first of these data visualization libraries that we are able to work with is Matplotlib.

This is going to be a library that is able to help us to really work on creating some 2D diagrams and graphs that we are working with.

This helps us to create a huge number of charts and graphs that we need to handle and show off some of the complex relationships that are going to show up in our work.

In addition, many of the other plotting libraries that are out there and pretty popular are designed so that they can work along with this Matplotlib.

There have been a lot of changes to Matplotlib over the years when it comes to the sizes, colors, legends, and fonts that we can work with.

These are good improvements to work with because they are going to show us a lot of different ways that we can create the graphs and more that we are looking at in a short amount of time.

We can also work with Seaborn.

This is going to be a higher-level of API that is going to be based on the Matplotlib library.

It is going to contain a more suitable default setting to help us to go through and process some of the charts that we want to work with.

There is also going to be a rich gallery of visuals that you are able to use, like the violin diagram, joint plots, and time series.

Programmers are able to work with the Plotly library as well.

This is going to be something that we are able to use when we would like an easy method to build up sophisticated graphics and more.

This is a package that is adapted to help work with web applications that are more interactive.

And it is going to include a lot of different visualizations that you are able to work with, including ternary plots, 3D plots, and contour graphics.

Machine Learning Libraries

As you go through this process and you work on some of the projects that come with data science, it is possible that you are going to work with machine learning as well.

You need to learn how to work with machine learning because it is going to help us to really see how to take that data and learn from it.

And this is where we are going to see some of that Python coding come into play.

With this in mind, some of the libraries that we are able to use that can help us use Python for machine learning will include:

Scikit-Learn is a library that we need to focus on.

This is going to be a module that works with Python and will be based on SciPy and NumPy and can be a great option to handle when it is time to work with data.

It is going to provide us with a ton of the algorithms that we need to work on machine learning and tasks of data mining, including model selection, dimensionality reduction, classification, regression, and clustering.

Deep Learning

Deep learning is going to be a subset of machine learning that takes some of the things that we are able to do with that to the next level.

A lot of the unsupervised machine learning tasks that you want to work with, and that we will talk about more later, will be done with the help of deep learning.

Some of the different tasks that we are able to handle when it comes to working on deep learning will include:

The first option is going to be TensorFlow.

This is going to be a very popular framework when it comes to machine learning and deep learning, and it was developed by Google Brain.

It is going to provide us with some abilities to work with multiple sets of data and neural networks all in one.

In fact, it is going to be one of the most popular deep learning options, and some of the applications of TensorFlow that you will be able to enjoy, including speech recognition, object identification, and more.

PyTorch is another framework that you are going to be able to work with, as well.

This is going to include a large framework that is going to allow us to perform some tensor computations with the help of CPU accelerations, create some dynamic computational graphs, and even calculate gradients automatically.

In addition to all of this, PyTorch is going to provide us with a rich API to help solve applications that are related to neural networks.

This is a library that is going to be based on Torch, which is another library that is open-sourced, deep learning, and implemented with the C language and a wrapper of Lua.

The Python API was not introduced until 2017, and from that point on, we are going to see that this is a framework that is really popular and used in many applications by data scientists.

The Keras library is next on the list.

This is going to be a library that is high-level that can help us with neural networks as well.

It is also going to be one that is able to work on top of Theano and TensorFlow.

It is going to be able to take some of the specific tasks that you need to spend your time on, and make them easier to handle while reducing how much monotonous code that you have to deal with in data science.

You will find that it is not going to be all that suitable for some of the more complicated things that you want to handle.

These are just a few of the different languages that you are going to be able to work with when it is time to handle all of the data science projects that you would like to work with.

Some of these are going to work well together, and others are not going to work the way that you want unless they are done on their own.

But often it is going to depend on the kind of project that you want to work with, and what you are hoping to get out of that process, for you to choose which of the libraries that you want to pick form.

The goal here is to learn about the libraries, know how your own project is supposed to work, and then move from there when it is time to make some choices on the library that you want to work with.

Chapter 4: Data Science and Applications

To some extent, data science is recently becoming the most popular field.

Nearly all of the world's businesses today use data science.

Consequently, the fuel of any industry is data science.

Industries that use data science include transport, banking, education, e-commerce, manufacturing, finance, and so on.

To this end, related to the convention of data science are various applications.

Multiple disciplines stem from this single career line.

With massive numbers of applications, data science has become quite essential for all industries.

It has shaped and kept so many businesses in any trends around the world.

It is not overnight that the function of data science applications develops.

Cheaper storage and computing have made tremendous contributions to shorten tasks people do in a day within a few hours.

It will be essential to discuss some of these critical applications and see how they have shaped today's industries.

Also, the way they transform the world and revolutionize people's perceptions of data.

Ultimately, it is vital to address various situations industries use data to make them better.

Banking and Finance

Finance takes the leading position when it comes to data science applications.

Every year, losses and bad debts were on the rise, and businesses were going down.

Grief was the order of the day for those surviving.

However, since they sanctioned loans while they have paperwork that provided them with various data, they needed rescue, and that is where data scientists came in to help.

As a vital element to match their competition, it is now more than a trend for the banking industries to engage in the applications of data science.

Right now, making smarter decisions, enhancing performance, and focusing their resources have been possible for banks because of those big data technologies.

Some of the cases of data science applications include:

Fraud Detection

For fraud involving credit cards prevention and detection, insurance, accounting, and so many more, data science application becomes crucial.

Banks are being proactive with the security of their employees and customers.

It is now faster for banks to resist activity on an account to minimize losses since they detect fraud quickly.

As a result, they have been able to avoid significant losses and achieve necessary protection when they implement a series of fraud detection schemes.

The fraud detection vital steps include:

- Estimation of model
- Getting data samplings for preliminary testing and model estimation
- Deployment and testing stage

Data scientists need to fine-tune and train individual data set since they are different.

There are demands for expertise in techniques of data-mining, including forecasting, classification, association, and clustering, to transform the in-depth theoretical knowledge into practical applications.

For example, the bank's fraud protection system can put unusual high transactions on hold pending confirmation from the account holder.

Algorithms of fraud detection can also investigate multiple accounts opened in a short period with the same data or unusual high purchases of popular items of new accounts.

Customer Data Management

It is part of the obligations of the banks to analyze, store, or collect vast numbers of data.

With these data, data science applications are transforming them into a possibility for banks to learn more about their customers.

Doing this will drive new revenue opportunities instead of seeing those data as a mere compliance exercise.

People widely use digital banking, and it is more popular these days.

The result of this influx produces terabytes of data by customers; therefore, isolating genuinely relevant data is the first line of action for data scientists.

With the customers' preferences, interactions, and behaviors, then, data science applications will isolate the information of the most relevant clients and process them to enhance the decision-making of the business.

Investment Banks Risk Modeling

While it serves the most critical purposes during the pricing of financial investments, investment banks have a high priority for risk modeling since it helps regulate commercial activities.

For investment goals and to conduct corporate reorganizations or restructuring, investment banking evaluates the values of businesses to facilitate acquisitions and mergers as well as create capital in corporate financing.

For banks, as a result, risk modeling seems exceedingly substantial, and with more data science tools in reserve and information at hand, they can assess it to their benefit.

Now, for efficient risk modeling and better data-driven decisions, with data science applications, innovators in the industry are leveraging these new technologies.

Personalized Marketing

Providing a customized offer that fits the preferences and needs of particular customers is crucial to success in marketing.

Now it is possible to make the right offer on the correct device to the right customer at the right time.

For a new product, people target selection to identify potential customers with the use of data science applications.

With the aid of apps, scientists create a model that predicts the probability of a customer's response to an offer or promotion through their demographics, historical purchase, and behavioral data.

Thus, banks have improved their customer relations, personalize outreach, and efficient marketing through data science applications.

Health and Medicine

An innovative potential industry to implement the solutions of data science in health and medicine.

From the exploration of genetic disease to the discovery of drugs and computerizing medical records, data analytics is taking medical science to an entirely new level.

It is perhaps astonishing that this dynamic is just the beginning.

Through finances, data science and healthcare are most times connected as the industry makes efforts to cut down on its expenses with the help of a large amount of data.

There is quite a significant development between medicine and data science, and their advancement is crucial.

Here are some of the impacts data science applications have on medicine and health.

Analysis of Medical Image

Medical imaging is one of the most significant benefits the healthcare sectors get from data science applications.

As significant research, Big Data Analytics in healthcare indicates that some of the imaging techniques in medicine and health are X-ray, magnetic resonance imaging (MRI), mammography, computed tomography, and so many others.

More applications in development will effectively extract data from images, present an accurate interpretation, and enhance the quality of the image.

As these data science applications suggest better treatment solutions, they also boost the accuracy of diagnoses.

Genomics and Genetics

Sophisticated therapy individualization is made possible through studies in genomics and genetics.

Finding the individual biological correlation between disease, genetics, and drug response and also understand the effect of the DNA on our health is the primary purpose of this study.

In the research of the disease, with an in-depth understanding of genetic issues in reaction to specific conditions and drugs, the integration of various kinds of data with genomic data comes through data science techniques.

It may be useful to look into some of these frameworks and technologies.

For a short time of processing efficient data, MapReduce allows reading genetic sequences mapping, retrieving genomic data is accessible through SQL, BAM file computation, and manipulation.

Also, principally to DNA interpretation to predict the molecular effects of genetic variation, Deep Genomics makes a substantial impact. Scientists have the ability to understand the manner in which genetic variations impact a genetic code with their database.

Drugs Creation

The process of drug discovery is highly complicated since it involves various disciplines.

Most times, the most excellent ideas pass through billions of enormous time and financial expenditure and testing.

Typically, getting a drug submitted officially can take up to twelve years.

With an addition of a perspective to the individual stage of drug compound screening to the prediction of success rate derived from the biological factors, the process is now shortened and simplified with the aid of data science applications.

Using simulations rather than the "lab experiments," and advanced mathematical modeling, these applications can forecast how the compound will act in the body.

With computational drug discovery, it produces simulations of computer models as a biologically relevant network simplifying the prediction of future results with high accuracy.

Virtual Assistance for Customer and Patients Support

The idea that some patients don't necessarily have to visit doctors in person is the concept behind the clinical process optimization.

Also, doctors don't necessarily have to visit too when the patients can get more effective solutions with the use of a mobile application.

Commonly as chatbots, the AI-powered mobile apps can provide vital healthcare support.

Derived from a massive network connecting symptoms to causes, it is as simple as receiving vital information about your medical condition after you describe your symptoms.

When necessary, applications can assign an appointment with a doctor and also remind you to take your medicine on time.

Alongside allowing doctors to have their focus on more critical cases, these applications save patients' time on waiting in line for an appointment as well as promote a healthy lifestyle.

Industry Knowledge

To offer the best possible treatment and improve the services, knowledge management in healthcare is vital.

It brings together externally generated information and internal expertise.

With the creation of new technologies and the rapid changes in the industry every day, effective distribution, storing, and gathering of different facts is essential.

For healthcare organizations to achieve progressive results, the integration of various sources of knowledge and their combined use in the treatment process is secure through data science applications.

Oil and Gas

The primary force behind various trends in industries like marketing, finance, internet, among others, is machine learning and data science.

And there appears to be no exception for the oil and gas industry through the extracting of important observations with some applications in the sectors in upstream, midstream, and downstream.

As a result, within the industry, a valuable asset to companies is refined data.

Data science applications are quite useful in some of these sectors of oil and gas.

Immediate Drag Calculation and Torque Using Neural Networks

There is a need to analyze, in drilling, the structured visual data, which operators get through logging.

Also, they can capture the electronic drilling recorder and contextual data, which takes the pattern of daily reports of the drilling log.

It is essential to make an instant decision because of the time-bound disposition of drilling operations.

As a result, companies predict drilling key performance indicators; analyze rig states for real-time data visualization with the use of neural networks.

Using the AI, they can estimate the coefficient of regular and friction contact forces between the wellbore and the string.

Also, in any given well, they can calculate on the drill strings real-time the drag and torque.

Historical data of pump washouts is what operators can utilize, and through the alerts on their phone, they will be able to know when and if there will be a washout.

Predicting Well Production Profile Through Feature Extraction Models

The recurring neural networks and time series forecasting are part of the optimization of oil and gas production.

Rates of gas-to-oil ratios and oil rates prediction are significant KPIs.

Operators can calculate bottom-hole pressure, choke, wellhead temperature, and daily oil rate prediction of data of nearby well with the use of feature extraction models.

In the event of predicting production decline, they make use of fractured parameters.

Also, for pattern recognition on sucker rod dynamometer cards, they utilize neural networks and deep learning.

Downstream Optimization

To process gas and crude oil, oil refineries use a massive volume of water.

Now, there is a system that tackles water solution management in the oil and gas industry.

Also, with the aid of distribution by analyzing data effectively, there is an increase in modeling speed for forecasting revenues through cloud-based services.

The Internet

Anytime anyone thinks about data science, the first idea that comes to mind is the internet.

It is typical of thinking of Google when we talk about searching for something on the internet.

However, Bing, Yahoo, AOL, Ask, and some others are also search engines.

For these search engines to give back to you in a fraction of a second when you put a search on them, data science algorithms are all that they all have in common.

Every day, Google processes more than 20 petabytes, and these search engines are known today with the help of data science.

Targeted Advertising

Of all the data science applications, the whole digital marketing spectrum is a significant challenge against the search engines.

The data science algorithms decide the distribution of digital billboards and banner displays on different websites.

And against the traditional advertisements, data science algorithms have helped marketers get higher click-through-rates.

Using the behavior of a user, they can target them with specific adverts.

At the same time and in the same place online, one user might see ads on anger management while another user sees another ad on a keto diet.

Website Recommendations

This case is something familiar to everyone as you see suggestions of the same products, even on eBay and Amazon.

Doing this adds so much to the user experience while it helps to discover appropriate products from several products available with them.

Leaning on the relevant information and interest of the users. So many businesses have promoted their products and services with this engine.

To improve user experience, some giants on the internet, including Google Play, Amazon, Netflix, and others, have used this system.

They derived these recommendations on the results of a user's previous search.

Advanced Image Recognition

The face recognition algorithm makes use of an automatic tag suggestion feature when a user uploads their picture on social media like Facebook and starts getting tag suggestions.

For some time now, Facebook has made significant capacity and accuracy with its image recognition.

Also, by uploading an image to the internet, you have the option of searching for them on Google, providing the results of related search with the use of image recognition.

Speech Recognition

Siri, Google Voice, Cortana, and so many others are some of the best speech recognition products.

It makes it easy for those who are not in the position of typing a message to use speech recognition tools.

Their speech will be converted to text when they speak out their words.

Though the accuracy of speech recognition is not certain.

Travel and Tourism

There are several constant challenges and changes, even with the exceptional opportunities data science has brought to many industries.

And there is no exception when it comes to travel and tourism.

Today, there is a rise in travel culture since a broader audience has been able to afford it.

Therefore, by getting more extensive than ever before, there is a dramatic change in the target market.

As a worldwide trend, travel and tourism is no more a privilege of the noble and the rich.

The data science algorithms have become essential in this industry to process massive data and also delight the requirements of the rising numbers of consumers.

To enhance their services every day, the hotels, airlines, booking and reservation websites, and several others now see big data are a vital tool.

The travel industry uses some of these tools to make it more efficient.

Customer Segmentation and Personalized Marketing

Personalization has become a preferred trend for some people to appreciate travel experience.

The customer segmentation is the general stack of services to please the needs of every group through the adaptation and segmenting of the customers according to their preferences.

Hence, finding a solution that will align with all situations is crucial.

Collecting users' social media data to unify behavior, metadata, and geolocation is what customer segmentation and personalized marketing is all about.

For the future, it assumes and processes the preferences of the user.

Analysis of Customer Sentiment

Recognizing emotional elements in the text and analyzing textual data is what sentiment analysis does.

The service provider, as well as the owner of a business, can learn about the customers' real attitude towards their brands through sentiment analysis.

The reviews of customers have a huge role when it comes to the travel industry.

This analysis is because to make decisions, travelers read reviews customers posted on various websites and platforms and then act upon these recommendations.

As a result, providing sentiment analysis is one of the service packages of some modern booking websites for those travel hotels and agencies that are willing to cooperate with them.

Recommendation Engine

This concept is one of the most promising and efficient, according to some experts.

In their everyday work, some central booking and travel web platforms use recommendation engines.

Mainly, through the available offers, they match the needs and wishes of customers with these recommendations.

Based on preferences and previous search, the travel and tourism companies have the ability to provide alternative travel dates, rental deals, new routes, attractions, and destinations when they apply the data-powered recommendation engine solutions.

Offering suitable provisions to all these customers, booking service providers and travel agencies achieve this with the use of recommendation engines.

Travel Support Bots

With the provisions of exceptional assistance in travel arrangements and support for the customers, travel bots are indeed changing the travel industry nowadays.

Saving user's money and time, answering questions, suggesting new places to visit, and organizing the trips have the influence of an AI-powered travel bot.

It is the best possible solution for customers' support due to its support of multiple languages and 24/7 accessibility mode.

It is significant to add that these bots are always learning and, as such, are becoming more helpful and smarter every day.

Therefore, solving the major tasks of travel and tourism is what a chatbot can do.

Both customers and business owners benefit from these chatbots.

Route Optimization

In the travel and tourism industry, route optimization plays a significant role.

It can be quite challenging to account for several destinations, plan trips, schedules, and working distances and hours.

With route optimization, it becomes easy to do some of the following:

- Time management
- Minimization of the travel costs
- Minimization of distance

For sure, data science improves lives and also continues to change the faces of several industries, giving them the opportunity of providing unique experiences for their customers with high satisfaction rates.

Apart from shifting our attitudes, data science has become one of the promising technologies that bring changes to different businesses.

With several solutions the data science applications provide, it is no doubt that its benefits cannot be over-emphasized.

Chapter 5: The Lifecycle of Data Science

The next thing that we need to take a look at here is the lifecycle of data science.

There are actually quite a few steps that we need to focus on here in order to make sure that we are going to get the most out of any data science project that we are trying to work with along the way.

It would be nice if it were a process that just took a few minutes, and then we were set, but this is just not how things are meant to go.

There are a lot of steps that have to all come together and work well together to ensure that this is going to work in the manner that we would like.

You have to make sure that you have the right data, for example, you have to make sure that you clean out the data and get it organized, and you need to run it through the algorithms and other models that you would like, just to learn what information and insights are found in all of that data.

This is a complex process that is going to take some time to accomplish, and often those who are just getting started with this process are going to be amazed at the amount of work that they have to use in order to make this happen for their needs.

Knowing the steps ahead of time will ensure that you are able to really get the most out of this process, that you will start out and end up in the right spot, and so much more. With that in mind, some of the steps that we need to use in order to get started with doing our own process of data science will include:

The Discovery Phase

The first phase of this that we need to take a look at is going to be the discovery phase.

This is going to include a lot of questions, a lot of research, and a good understanding of what your business is hoping to get out of this whole process before we even get started.

Before you even think about starting out on this project, it is important to go through and understand some of the different specifications, the requirements, and then the priorities and the required budget to make this all work.

Going in without all of this in place is just going to lead to a mess.

If you do not have an idea of what the specifications and priorities are supposed to be in this process, then you are just going to grab any random data that you can find, and that is easy to gather up, and then call it good.

This will definitely not be a good thing for what you are trying to do.

If you do not go into this knowing the budget, the money will run out way before you are able to figure out how this process even works.

You need to make sure in this stage that you have the right ability in order to ask the right questions all of the time. Here, you will assess if you have the right resources at hand, as well.

This means that you need to know whether you have the right amount of data, time, technology, and people in order to fully support the project that you are working with.

And finally, we have to be able to frame our main business problem (or at least the one that we want to work with right now) and formulate an initial hypothesis to test it all out.

The Data Preparation Phase

The next thing that we need to take a look at is the data preparation phase.

This is going to be the phase where you will spend most of your time in because we have to make sure that we are not just gathering up the right information as we go along.

We want to make sure that we are organizing the data, dealing with the outliers that are there, filling in the missing values, and being careful about the duplicates that are going to show up in this process as well.

It is a difficult task to work with, but it is necessary if we would like to make sure that our predictions are going to be as accurate as possible.

This is not the most glamorous out of the work that you are doing, but it is very important.

In this phase, it is often necessary that we have an analytical sandbox in which we are able to perform some of the analytics for the entire time that we work on the project at hand.

We need to spend some time in this stage looking and exploring the data, preprocessing it, and conditioning the data before we do the modeling.

This all takes time, and it may not be fun, but it is something that is necessary when it comes to the success of your project.

In addition, during this phase, we are going to work with the process known as ETLT, or extract, transform, load, and transform in order to make sure that the data is organized and ready to go in the manner that we would like and to make sure that we are able to get the data into the sandbox that we would like.

There are going to be a few different options that we are able to work on in order to handle the data preparation phase that we are on right now.

The two most popular options and the ones that will ensure that we are able to get the most out of the process will be the R and the Python coding language.

For the most part, data scientists are going to use Python in order to get the most out of their training process.

Working with Python is the best choice.

It is simple enough to learn how to use, even for someone who is more of a beginner in all of this, and it will ensure that you have all of the power and all of the libraries that are needed in order to handle this phase as well.

There are a lot of different parts that we are going to focus on when it is time to handle the data preparation phase of the whole process.

And often, it is a phase that we are not going to spend enough time on.

But in reality, if the data that you have is not organized and ready to go in the manner that you would like, then it is going to cause a lot of problems along the way.

The cleaner that you are able to make that data, the better.

When the data is higher in quality, and when things like the outliers, duplicates, and missing values are gone, it is so much easier to work with all of this.

The algorithm will be able to go through the data more efficiently than before, and you will have predictions and insights that you are actually able to handle and trust along the way as well.

The Model Planning Phase

The third step that we are going to be able to work with is known as the model planning phase.

In this one, we are going to spend some time determining the techniques and methods that are available in order to draw up the relationships between the variables that we have.

These relationships are important because they are basically going to help us set the foundation for the algorithms that we want to implement.

Without these algorithms, your coding is not going to work, and you will never learn what is inside of that data you are dealing with.

And we will learn how to implement some of these algorithms in the next phase.

There are a number of planning tools that are available for us to work with on this one.

Most programmers are going to focus on the Python language and all of the benefits that it is able to provide.

There are a few others that we are able to spend our time and attention on, and these will include:

- **R:** This one is sometimes seen as the best option to work with when it comes to completing a data analysis because it allows us to have the capabilities of modeling and will provide us with a really good environment when it is time to build up the interpretive models that we want.

- **SQL Analysis Services:** These are going to be the ones that are able to perform some of the analytics that need to happen in the database.

  These are going to be done thanks to some of the more common functions of data mining, as long as they are used with some of the basic predictive models that you need as well.

- **SAS/ACCESS:** This one is going to be helpful because we are able to use it to access all of the data that we need from the Hadoop system when we need it the most.

  And it is often going to be used when we would like to create model flow diagrams that we can repeat, and that we are able to reuse in the process as well.

At this point, we should have a really good idea about some of the nature of our data, and we should know whether it is to the quality standards that we are looking for or not.

And because of this, it is time to move on to the next step and ensure that we are ready to handle some of the data by putting it through the algorithms that we pick in the next step.

This is where we are heading in the next step as well, it will be time to add in a bit of machine learning (which we are going to be able to use in more depth later on when we discuss it), in order to find a good algorithm that will go through the data that we have, and will provide us with the insights and predictions that we need.

But this is only going to happen when we are able to go through and do some of the steps that were listed out before.

The Model Building Phase

The fourth step that we need to take some time on here is going to be the model-building phase.

When we are here, we will need to actually go through and use machine learning and some of the algorithms that are necessary with it and put it to good use.

This is also the phase where we are going to find all of the data sets and more that we need to handle the training and the testing.

One thing that a lot of people are not aware of when they first get started with all of this is that they actually need to go through and train and then test the algorithm.

They assume that they are able to just write out the algorithm in the manner that they would like, and then put through the data that they want.

They then assume that the data that comes out of these untrained and untested algorithms are going to be accurate and will actually help them out with the work that they want to do.

But these algorithms have to be trained in some manner, and if you do not take the time to do this training ahead of time, or you don't take the time to test them out either, then you are going to end up with some trouble.

The algorithm is not going to be as accurate as we would like, and we will end up with a lot of predictions and insights that we are not able to trust at all.

During this phase, we will also need to take some time to discover or consider whether the tools that we already have in our possession are going to be enough to help run some of those models, or if we are going to need to make sure that the environment that we are working with will be more robust.

Usually, when we take a look at this, we are interested in finding out whether the processing power that we have is strong enough to handle the work or if we need to change it up.

The good news here is that there are a lot of great algorithms that we are able to use to make this one work, and when we are able to put them all together and use all of the tools that are out there, you will be able to create some really good information that will push you forward.

But you have to take the time to really optimize the algorithm that you want to work with and to ensure that it is going to be able to handle some of the predictions and insights that we need to make all of this work for our needs.

The Operationalize Phase

When we are working with this phase, it is time to deliver some of the final reports and briefings, as well as some of the codes and technical documents that are needed to go along with this one.

Usually, the data scientist will need to spend their time showing the right people in the business how to work on the information and make it work for their needs as well.

And since a lot of these key decision-makers are often not going to have technical backgrounds, understanding the information is going to be tough.

This is why the data scientist will need to spend some time going through the information and getting it set up in a manner that will make it easier overall.

When the data is turned into a format that we are able to understand, and will ensure those who are using the information for making decisions, then it is going to help them out quite a bit.

In addition, sometimes we are going to take some time to work on a pilot project.

This can be implemented in real-time in the production environment as well.

This allows us to take some time to try out some of the insights that we have found, without having to implement them throughout the whole company.

This gives us a better idea of what is going on with some of the work that we are doing, and to see whether the process we want to use is going to actually work before we waste time and money on doing it throughout the company.

This is one of the best ways for us to go through and see a clear picture of the performance and other related constraints on a smaller scale before you deploy it completely.

The Communicate Results Phase

At this point, it is important for us to go through and evaluate whether or not we have been able to achieve some of our goals.

This is talking about some of the goals that we were able to go through in the first phase of this process.

If we have not been able to gather up and work with the goals along the way, then we will be able to work with making some of the necessary changes that will help us to meet our goals.

So, when we are in this last phase, we are going to spend some time identifying all of the key findings that are going to show up along the way.

And when we have been able to identify some of these key findings, we can then communicate that information between the stakeholders, and then determine whether or not the results of this project are going to be a failure, or if we were successful.

But we have to base all of this on the criteria that we took the time to develop and look at in the first phase.

As we can see, there is quite a bit that is going to show up when it is time to handle some of the work that we need with a data science project.

We have to go through all of these phases to ensure that we are going to see some of the best results along the way.

And when it all comes together, we will be able to have the right data, that we are cleaning it off, and that we are picking out the right algorithms to ensure that this is going to work the way that we would like.

Chapter 6: Probability, Statistics, and Data Types

Things are quite straightforward in Knowledge Representation and Reasoning; KR&R.

Exclusive of doubt, formulating and representing propositions is easy.

The thing is, when uncertainty makes itself known, problems begin to arise—for example, an expert system designed to replace a doctor.

For diagnosing patients, a doctor possesses no formal knowledge of treating the patient and no official rules based on symptoms.

In this situation, to determine if the patient has a specific condition and also the cure for it, it is the probability the expert system will use to formulate the highest probability chance.

Real-Life Probability Examples

As a mathematical term, probability has to do with the possibility that an event may occur, like taking out from a bag of assorted colors a piece of green or drawing an ace from a deck of cards.

In all daily decision-making processes, you use probability even without having a clue of the consequences.

While you may determine the best course of action is to make judgment calls using subjective probability, you may not perform actual probability problems sometimes.

Organize Around the Weather

You can make plans with the weather in mind since you use probability almost every day.

Predicting the weather condition is not possible for meteorologists and, as a result, to establish the possibility that there will be snow, hail, or rain, they utilize instruments and tools.

For example, it has rained with the conditions of the weather that is 60 out of 100 days amid the same conditions when there is a 60 percent chance of rain.

Intuitively, rather than going to work with an umbrella or putting on sandals, closed-toed shoes, maybe preferred outfit to wear.

Also, not only do meteorologists analyze probable weather patterns for that week or day, but with the historical databases that they also examine to calculate approximately low and high temperatures.

Strategies in Sports

For competitions and games, the probability is what coaches and athletes utilize to influence the best strategies for sports.

When putting any player in the lineup, a coach of baseball evaluates the batting average of such a player.

For example, out of every ten at-bats, an athlete may get a base hit two if the player's batting average is 200.

The odds are even higher for a player to even have, out of every ten at-bats, four hits when such a player has a 400-batting average.

Another example is when; with field goal attempts from over 40 yards out of 15, a high-school football kicker makes nine in a season, his next goal effort from the same space may be about 60 percent chance.

We can have an equation like this:

9/15 = 0.60 or 60 percent

Insurance Option

To conclude on the plans that are best for your family and even for you and the required deductible amounts, probability plays a vital role in analyzing insurance policies.

For example, you make use of probability to know how possible it can be that you will need to make a declaration when you choose a car insurance policy.

You may likely make consideration for not only liability but comprehensive insurance on your car when 12 percent or of every

100 drivers over the past year, 12 out of them in your community have crashed into a deer.

Also, if following a deer-connected event run $28,000, not to be in a situation where you cannot afford to cover certain expenses, you might consider a lower deductible on car repairs.

Recreational and Games Activities

Probability is what you use when you engage in video or card games or play board games that have the involvement of chance or luck.

A required video game covert missile or the chances of getting the cards you need in poker is what you must weigh.

Also, the determination of the extent of the risk you will be eager to take rests on the possibility of getting those tokens or cards.

For example, as Wolfram Math World suggests, getting three of a class in a poker hand is the odds of 46.3-to-1, about a chance of 2 percent.

However, you will have about 42 percent or 1.4-to-1 odds that you will catch one pair.

It is through the help of probability that you settle on the manner with which you intend to play the game when you assess what is at stake.

Statistics

The basis of modern science is on the statements of probability and statistical significance.

In one example, according to studies, cigarette smokers have a 20 times greater likelihood of developing lung cancer than those who don't smoke.

In another research, the next 200,000 years will have the possibility of a catastrophic meteorite impact on Earth.

Also, against the second male children, the first-born male children exhibit IQ test scores of 2.82 points.

But, why do scientists talk in ambiguous expressions?

Why don't they say; that lung cancer is a result of cigarette smoking?

And they could have informed people if there needs to be an establishment of a colony on the moon to escape the disaster of the extraterrestrial.

The rationale behind these recent analyses is an accurate reflection of the data.

It is not common to have absolute conclusions in scientific data.

Some smokers can reduce the risk of lung cancer if they quit, while some smokers never contract the disease; other than lung cancer, it was cardiovascular diseases that kill some smokers prematurely.

As a form of allowing scientists to make more accurate statements about their data, it is the statistic function to quantify variability since there is an exhibition of variability in all data.

Those statistics offer evidence that something is incorrect may be a common misconception.

However, statistics have no such features.

Instead, to observe a specific result, they provide a measure of the probability.

Scientists can put numbers to probability through statistical techniques, taking a step away from the statement that someone is more likely to develop lung cancer if they smoke cigarettes to a report that says it is nearly 20 times greater in cigarette smokers compared to nonsmokers for the probability of developing lung cancer.

It is a powerful tool the quantification of probability statistics offers and scientists use it thoroughly, yet they frequently misunderstand it.

Statistics in Data Analysis

Developed for data analysis is a large number of procedures for statistics they are in two parts of inferential and descriptive:

Descriptive Statistics: With the use of measures for deviation like mean, median, and standard, scientists have the capability of quickly summing up significant attributes of a dataset through descriptive statistics.

They allow scientists to put the research within a broad context while offering a general sense of the group they study.

For example, initiated in 1959, potential research on mortality was Cancer Prevention Study 1 (CPS-1).

Among other variables, investigators gave reports of demographics and ages of the participants to let them compare, at the time, the United States' broader population and also the study group.

The age of the volunteers was from ages 30 to 108, with age in the middle as 52 years.

The research had 57 percent female as subjects, 2 percent black, and 97 percent white.

Also, in 1960, the total population of females in the US was 51 percent, black was about 11 percent, and white was 89 percent.

The statistics of descriptive easily identified CPS-1's recognized shortcomings by suggesting that the research made no effort to sufficiently consider illness profiles in the US marginal groups when 97 percent of participants were white.

Inferential Statistics: When scientists want to make a considered opinion about data, making suppositions about bigger populaces with the use of smaller samples of data, discover the connection between variables in datasets, and model patterns in data, they make use of inferential statistics.

From the perspective of statistics, the term "population" may differ from the ordinary, meaning that it belongs to a collection of people.

The larger group is a geometric population used by a dataset for making suppositions about a society, locations of an oil field, meteor impacts, corn plants, or some various sets of measurements accordingly.

With regard to scientific studies, the process of shifting results to larger populations from small sample sizes is quite essential.

For example, though there was the conscription of about 1 million and 1.2 million individuals in that order for the Cancer Prevention Studies I and II, their representation is for a tiny portion of the 1960 and 1980 United States people that totaled about 179 and 226 million.

Correlation, testing/point estimation, and regression are some of the standard inferential techniques.

For example, Tor Bjerkedal and Peter Kristensen analyzed 250,000 male's test scores in IQ for personnel of the Norwegian military in 2007.

According to their examination, the IQ test scores of the first-born male children scored higher points of 2.82 +/- 0.07 than second-born male children, a 95 percent confidence level of a statistical difference.

The vital concept in the analysis of data is the phrase "statistically significant," and most times, people misunderstand it.

Similar to the frequent application of the term *significant*, most people assume that a result is momentous or essential when they call it significant.

However, the case is different.

Instead, an estimate of the probability is the statistical significance that the difference or observed association is because of chance instead of any actual connection.

In other words, when there is no valid existing difference or link, statistical significance tests describe the probability that the difference or a temporary link would take place.

Because it has a similar implication in statistics typical of regular verbal communication, though people can measure it, the measure of significance is most times expressed in terms of confidence.

Data Types

To do Exploratory Data Analysis, EDA, you need to have a clear grasp of measurement scales, which are also the different data types because specific data types have correlated with the use of individual statistical measurements.

Additionally, to select the precise visualization process, there is the requirement of identifying data types with which you are handling.

The manner with which you can categorize various types of variables is data types.

Now, let's take an in-depth look at the main types of variables and their examples, and we may refer to them as measurement scales sometimes.

Categorical Data

Characteristics are the representation of categorical data.

As a result, it stands for things such as someone's language, gender, and so on.

Also, numerical values have a connection with categorical data like 0 for females and 1 for regard.

Be aware that those numbers have no mathematical meaning.

Nominal Data

The discrete units are the representation of nominal values, and they use them to label variables without any quantitative value.

They are nothing but "labels." It is important to note that nominal data has no order.

Hence, nothing would change about the meaning even if you improve the order of its values.

For example, the value may not change when a question is asking you for your gender, and you need to choose between female and male.

The order has no value.

Ordinal Data

Ordered and discrete units are what ordinal values represent.

Except for the importance of its ordering, ordinal data is therefore almost similar to nominal data.

For example, when a question asks you about your educational background and has the order of elementary, high school, undergraduate, and graduate.

If you observe, there is a difference between college and high school and also between high school and elementary.

Here is where the major limitation of ordinal data suffices; it is hard to know the differences between the values.

Due to this limitation, they use ordinal scales to measure non-numerical features such as customer satisfaction, happiness, etc.

Numerical Data

Discrete Data: When its values are separate and distinct, then we refer to discrete data.

In other words, when the data can take on specific benefits, then we speak of discrete data.

It is possible to count this type of data, but we cannot measure it.

Classification is the category that its information represents.

A perfect instance is the number of heads in 100-coin flips.

To know if you are dealing with discrete data or not, try to ask the following two questions: can you divide it into smaller and smaller parts, or can you count it?

Continuous Data: Measurements are what continuous data represents, and as such, you can only measure them, but you can't count their values.

For example, with the use of intervals on the real number lines, you can describe someone's height.

Interval Data: The representation of ordered units with similar differences is interval values.

Consequently, in the course of a variable that contains ordered numeric values and where we know the actual differences between the values is interval data.

For example, a feature that includes a temperature of a given place may have the temperature in -10, -5, 0, +5, +10, and +15. Interval values have a setback since they have no "true zero."

It implies that there is no such thing as the temperature in regards to the example.

Subtracting and adding is possible with interval data.

However, they don't give room for division, calculation, or multiplication of ratios.

Ultimately, it is hard to apply plenty of inferential and descriptive statistics because there is no true zero.

Ratio Data: Also, with a similar difference, ratio values are ordered units.

The contrast of an absolute zero is what ratio values have, the same as the interval values.

For example, weight, length, height, and so on.

The Importance of Data Types

Since scientists can only use statistical techniques with specific data types, then data types are an essential concept.

You may have a wrong analysis if you continue to analyze data differently than categorical data.

As a result, you will have the ability to choose the correct technique of study when you have a clear understanding of the data with which you are dealing.

It is essential to go over every data once more. However, in regards to what statistic techniques one can apply.

There is a need to understand the basics of descriptive statistics before you can comprehend what we have to discuss right now.

Note: You can read all about descriptive statistics down the line in this chapter.

Statistical Methods

Nominal Data

The sense behind dealing with nominal data is to accumulate information with the aid of:

- **Frequencies:** The degree upon which an occasion takes place concerning a dataset or over a period is the frequency.

- **Proportion:** When you divide the frequency by the total number of events, you can easily calculate the proportion. For example, how often an event occurs divided by how often the event could occur.

- **Percentage:** Here, the technique required is visualization, and a bar chart or a pie chart is all that you need to visualize nominal data. To transform nominal data into a numeric feature, you can make use of one-hot encoding in data science.

Ordinal Data

The same technique you use in nominal data can be applied with ordinal data.

However, some additional tools are there for you to access.

Consequently, proportions, percentages, and frequencies are the data you can use for your summary.

Bar charts and pie charts can be used to visualize them.

Also, for the review of your data, you can use median, interquartile range, mode, and percentiles.

Continuous Data

You can use most techniques for your data description when you are dealing with continuous data.

For the summary of your data, you can use range, median, percentiles, standard deviation, interquartile range, and mean.

Visualization Techniques: A box-plot or a histogram, checking the variability, central tendency, kurtosis of a distribution, and modality all come to mind when you are attempting to visualize continuous data.

You need to be aware that when you have any outliers, a histogram may not reveal that.

That is the reason for the use of box-plots.

Descriptive Statistics

As an essential aspect of machine learning, to have an understanding of your data, you need descriptive statistical analysis since making predictions is what machine learning is all about.

On the other hand, as a necessary initial step, you conclude from data through statistics.

Your dataset needs to go through descriptive statistical analysis.

Most people often get to wrong conclusions by losing a considerable amount of beneficial understandings regarding their data since they skip this part.

It is better to be careful when running your descriptive statistics, take your time, and for further analysis, ensure your data complements all prerequisites.

Normal Distribution

Since almost all statistical tests require normally distributed data, the most critical concept of statistics is the normal distribution.

When scientists plot it, it is essentially the depiction of the patterns of large samples of data. Sometimes, they refer to it as the "Gaussian curve" or the "bell curve."

There is a requirement that a normal distribution is given for calculation and inferential statistics of probabilities.

The implication of this is that you must be careful of what statistical test you apply to your data if it is not normally distributed since they could lead to wrong conclusions.

If your data is symmetrical, unimodal, centered, and bell-shaped, a normal distribution is given.

Each side is an exact mirror of the other in a perfectly normal distribution.

Central Tendency

Mean, mode, and the median is what we need to tackle in statistics.

Also, these three are referred to as the "Central Tendency."

Apart from being the most popular, these three are distinctive "averages."

With regard to its consideration as a measure that is most consistent with the central propensity for formulating a hypothesis about a population from a particular model, the mean is the average.

For the clustering of your data value around its mean, mode, or median, central tendency determines the tendency.

When the values' number is divided, the mean is computed by the sum of all values.

The category or value that frequently happens contained by the data is the mode.

When there is no repletion of number or similarity in the class, there is no mode in a dataset.

Also, it is likely for a dataset to have more than one mode.

For categorical variables, the single central tendency measure is the mode since you can compute, such as the variable "gender" average.

Percentages and numbers are the only categorical variables you can report.

Also known as the "50th percentile," the midpoint or "middle" value in your data is the median.

More than the mean, the median is much less affected by skewed data and outliers.

For example, when a housing prizes dataset is from $100,000 to £300,000 yet has more than $3 million worth of houses.

Divided by the number of values and the sum of all values, the expensive homes will profoundly impact the mean.

As all data points "middle" value, these outliers will not profoundly affect the median.

Consequently, for your data description, the median is a much more suited statistic.

Chapter 7: Most Common Data Science Problems

Regardless of whether you pursue a full-time job in the field, or if you're using data analytics in your pre-existing career, you'll face certain problems with your work.

You can't always have a flawless and efficient workflow, no-one can, if you could, you'd soon enough become obsolete because there'd be countless people like you.

While some parts of working in data science are utterly amazing, there are still some issues.

You can easily get frustrated, especially since most of your superiors won't know in detail what you do.

It's very difficult to communicate with non-data-analysts precisely what you do.

Because of this, the post is prone to misunderstandings and mismanagement.

While all that's true, some of the problems you'll have can be managed and resolved.

In this section, we'll look at the most common complaints that people working with data analytics have had in the past, as well as how to resolve them without much consequence.

Management Expects the World

This issue is especially prevalent in positions that require you to do a degree in data modeling.

Most data modeling concerns gathering and cleaning the data so that it's actually usable.

This is obviously quite a bit of an issue on the manager's fault, as many of them will just suddenly come up with an idea and expect it to be done last-minute.

Obviously, sometimes the modelers are at fault, but unfortunately, more often than not, it's managers simply not understanding the job.

In the management world, it's quite common to insert things last-minute, but in data analytics that's basically impossible.

Your manager might just pop in and say, "Hey, we're going to include a social media history in our latest analysis. Cool? Cool, I'll see you in 15 minutes when it's done."

Now, if you sigh at this kind of request, then at least there are some solutions for it.

Not resolving this issue is bound to either cause serious delays, or some serious dissatisfaction from your managers.

The worst thing here is that both sides of the argument are entirely understandable.

The data scientists simply can't deal with this in such a short time span, and managers will have a hard time understanding that.

Serious complaints about managers being unreasonable and expecting the world are quite common in most technical fields, especially those concerning programming and AI.

Fortunately, some solutions exist, and most of them are concerned with improving your communication skills while at the same time being clear about the possibilities of what is possible, and what isn't.

Let's run through some solutions now.

First of all, you should keep communication open, but keep a firm "no changes" date.

After that date, make sure your manager is aware no changes will be processed.

Unfortunately, some managers will not be swayed by this.

Be clear about what you can or cannot do.

You can't expect your manager to be perfectly well versed in data analytics.

The main mistake managers make here is expecting data scientists to utilize datasets that either contain bad, little, or no data and actually have something to show for it at the end of the day.

It's imperative to explain to your manager what you can and cannot do.

Give them a few useful articles to read about what ML and AI can actually accomplish, rather than what they've probably read.

These days ML and AI are being hyped up to be essentially omnipotent and capable of turning any dataset into extremely valuable information.

Unfortunately, as you know, this is quite far from the truth.

The analysis you make has a limit on how good it can be, and that limit is the quality of the data you're given.

Naturally, you can use interpolation and extrapolation to "plug" the holes in a dataset, but it's not like there's a magic wand you can just point at the computer to create data.

If you're given a week of sales info, it doesn't matter how good you are; you won't be able to predict the sales of next year accurately.

The best thing you can do about this is to pay attention to what kind of company you apply to.

Do they already have many data scientists onboard?

Do they collect a lot of good data already?

Are they maybe adaptable enough to start collecting it as soon as you join?

If the answer to these questions is no, you might want to reconsider working there.

It's important to address this early on so it doesn't affect you in the future.

Besides that, try to explain to your manager that last-minute alterations are very difficult, and try to use phrases like "Yes, I could totally do that, it's just going to add about options days to the schedule."

Your manager's going to be singing a different tune soon.

Misunderstanding How Data Works

Generally, people think of data as a set of information, a truth if you will.

This couldn't be farther from the truth.

Data is merely facts until someone comes by and puts some context into it.

This is an issue that can affect basically everyone; your boss, your manager, even you might fall into this faulty mindset.

Being careful not to think about data as the information is one of the most crucial parts of being a data analytics expert.

Fundamentally, it's extremely important to remember that even if your title is "data analyst" when it comes to actual work, the analyst comes before the data.

Fostering a data-first culture in the workplace is a surefire way to have every one of your endeavors heralded by utter failure.

It's easy to forget that data needs context to be useful, and it is so, so easy to fall down the slippery slope of worshiping data.

Giving the context is your job; your job is to think about the data, to frame it.

The data itself is like a wench is to a mechanic.

You don't go praising the wench for fixing the car, so you shouldn't rely on the data too much either.

You need to know the broader conditions; for example, market trends that aren't in the data need to be considered.

While your managers might be most inclined to trust in the numbers, your job is to reveal where those numbers might be faulty, what might be affecting them, and what the truth is closest to.

Fortunately, this is an easy problem to solve; just let them have it.

If your manager gets burned for a few million because they trusted data more than you, then next time, you can be sure that they're going to pay more attention to your words next time around.

Now, you also need to consider the bias of data collection when dealing with work.

All data collection processes are susceptible to certain biases.

Let's say that you're analyzing a market based on how many people buy from the company site.

In this case, the bias is on younger, more tech-savvy people, as older people are more likely to buy from brick-and-mortar stores.

Taking the Blame for Bad News

Unfortunately, when it comes to being a data scientist, your recommendations are likely to end up in one of three ways: A bonus, a promotion, or expulsion from work.

The danger of working as anyone that concerns themselves with data analytics is that you will often have to profess the bad news to your bosses.

Unfortunately, not all of them have read Sun Tzu's book of war and refuse to shoot the messenger.

If your data analysis shows that there are serious problems in the company, or even that the company is headed towards its own destruction, it's quite likely your bosses will be less than kind.

Presenting this information can feel very awkward and uncomfortable, and can sometimes end up in disastrous consequences.

In most cases, you won't be to blame for this, but you are an easy link to scapegoat.

Any manager can easily put the blame on you, and your boss might not be well versed enough to see through it.

Now, ultimately, this is an issue you cannot precisely solve.

If your boss is blaming you for what you found out after digging through the company data, you'll probably want to check if your resume is up to date as soon as possible.

You don't need, and shouldn't put up with being attacked for doing your job.

If you're really committed to solving the issue, try assigning blame to yourself.

You can't hold your job if you sidestep telling your boss about things that were others' responsibilities.

Even if companies are trying to be modern and adapt to changes in the industry swiftly, fundamentally, most companies still run in an old-fashioned manner.

The complaint that Strand has articulated is extremely common in data scientists, and the chances that you aren't going to run into an example of this in your career are close to nil.

A recent study has shown that ⅔ of all managers distrust data and would rather hand over decision-making onto their intuition rather than trusting scientists.

Unfortunately, these are generally mid-level managers, who have just enough power to feel like they're important, but not enough power to affect the decisions made on a broader, company-wide scale.

Most data scientists get stuck with working for one of these at least at one point in their careers.

You'll find that you have to convince the management of practically every new decision you have to make.

Do you need better data collection?

Are you trying to make a financial model of the company spending so you can budget accordingly?

Well, too bad, because Steve from management has decided that his intuition tops that.

Even in the case that you've actually gotten approval for your project, you'll still face challenges with getting management to well... Act accordingly.

Even if your model showed that your company spends too much on marketing, good luck convincing your managers of that.

This is why skills in communications are so useful for any role related to data science. All of the analytical skills in the world are going to be useless if there's nobody to take action upon them.

Your results won't have even the slightest impact on the firm unless you're able to engage upper management enough with your speech, data presentation, etc.

This is why it's important to keep in mind soft skills, as well as your ability to do presentations and visualizations of projects.

It's much easier to convince management if you're showing them shapes and figures, rather than Excel spreadsheets.

Try running your presentation by a friend that has absolutely no technical skills; this will prove to you whether your presentation is fine.

Pay attention to what questions are posed to you, and try to address them more clearly in the presentation.

It's also sometimes useful to try to explain your ideas to an inanimate object.

This lets you pay attention to how you talk as well as how you communicate the data without the need to have an actual person with you there.

With that being said, don't feel too bad if it doesn't work out.

Sometimes your managers will simply elect not to listen to the data or decide that something is simply more important.

A relatively recent case of this was when data analytics showed that Grace & Frankie's promotional images worked the best without the show's star.

The team of executives at Netflix then had to think about the pros and cons of excluding the lead, Jane Fonda, from the images.

In the end, they elected not to, partly not to anger the lead, and partly because the show would be more "iconic" if the lead was present, rather than if promotional images were used exclusively as an advertisement.

The only fortunate thing here is that this is a bit of a cascading issue.

If you fail a few times, management is unlikely ever to trust you again.

On the other hand, if you bring success a few times, you'll build their confidence in your data, and they'll be much more likely to trust you with important projects.

It is a matter of picking your battles, so to speak, try to only engage where you are absolutely sure you can succeed.

Communication as a Solution

You might have noticed that the overarching theme here is communication, and it is.

While your data analytics and portfolio are the things that will let you get the job and perform it well, mere performance isn't enough.

To make your day-to-day life better and your career more successful, you have to practice communication and learn how to speak to your managers in the most effective ways possible.

If you're looking to hone your communication skills, look no further than those same managers you take issue with.

They tend to be quite good at communicating with their bosses, talking to them, and paying attention to the terms and tactics they use can be an excellent way to learn communication skills.

Above all, it is important to practice.

Try to make your every email sound more professional, your every message to be more concise and effective.

The same way you analyze in your job, analyze your approach to your job, think about what the most effective words to use are, and when to use them.

Chapter 8: Comparison of Python with Other Languages

Python can be compared with other high-level programming languages.

In comparison to other languages, Python surpasses based on functionalities, methods, libraries, and user-friendliness.

This language has professional modules, frameworks, and translators that are increasing its popularity among the software industry and IT professionals.

These correlations focus on the credibility of programming code and other significant factors. Let's discuss the detailed comparison of Python with other programming languages.

Python versus Java comparison

Java programs are faster than Python programs.

Python is vastly improved as a "high-level" language, while Java is better described as a low-level execution language.

Indeed, the two together make a superb mixture.

Various segments can be generated in Java and joined to shape usage in Python.

Python can be utilized to model parts until their structure can be "solidified" in Java usage.

A Python program written in Java is considered half-developed, which permits calling Python code from Java and the other way around.

In this execution, Python source code is meant Java bytecode (with assistance from a runtime library to help Python's dynamic semantics).

Java is a carefully embodied language, which means the variable names must be unequivocally proclaimed. Interestingly, we have a progressively composed Python, where no affirmation is required.

There are numerous questions about powerful and measurement producing in programming languages.

Notwithstanding, one idea ought to be noted: Python is an adaptable language with a straightforward sentence structure, which makes it a superb answer for composing contents and rapidly creating applications for different fields.

Java enables you to make cross-platform applications, while Python is good with practically all cutting-edge working frameworks.

Regarding start, Java is unreasonably convoluted for tenderfoots contrasted with Python.

Furthermore, the simplicity of perusing code is better with Python.

When you require your code to be executed from anyplace, at that point, pick Java.

The other bit of leeway of Java is that it gives you a chance to make organized-based applications, while Python can't.

Java is considerably more convoluted than Python. When you don't have any specialized foundation learning, Java won't be simple.

Then again, Java is utilized to program for various conditions and runtime executions of the program.

Python versus C#

Regarding effortlessness, Python was initially made to look like English discourse.

Such vast numbers of articulations in it are anything but difficult to peruse, mainly if you utilize appropriate variable names.

Moreover, because of basic grammar, there are no entangled developments, for example, syntactic sections, countless word-modifiers, different C-like developments, and various approaches to introducing factors.

Everything makes the code written in Python simple for comprehension and learning.

Simultaneously, C#, because of the language heredity, has loads of things from C++ and Java, which is at first communicated in C-like sentence structure.

Also, the C# language structure makes it essential to adhere to specific standards when composing your techniques or acquiring classes, which is joined by another surge of word-modifiers.

One shouldn't likewise disregard squares of code, which ought to be 'enclosed' in props.

Python doesn't have everything; it uses shifts which additionally make the code look perfect.

Concerning the code programming composition, it's likely worth referencing that projects which Python calls code are codes; they are merely recording with code that can be effectively executed by the mediator.

One can open them in any manager, work with them, and after that, quickly run once more.

Also, with Python, it's a lot simpler to compose cross-platform contents that should be recompiled.

In the Python programming language, we can design the required function to translate the code by machine and can shift this code to other platforms or systems to get executed.

This cross-platform feature of this programming language is unique.

Subsequently, it will build the size of the content from a few kilobytes to twelve megabytes.

Not helpful for one-time use.

Thus, C# requires IDE for typical programming. As one or more of C#, it has a reliable help for different segments of the Windows framework when you are composing content for Windows.

For instance, there are worked in devices for working with the library, WMI, the system, etc.

Also, C# enables you to utilize WinForms, which makes it extremely simple to create a graphical interface if it is all of a sudden, required all things considered.

There is no right answer to what language Python or C# is better.

Python is simpler to learn; it has a lot of increasingly open-source libraries contrasted with C#.

However, the standard library of C# is superior to Python's, C# has more functions, its presentation is higher, and it advances truly quick.

Python versus JavaScript

Python's "object-based" subset is commonly corresponding to JavaScript.

Like JavaScript (and not at all like Java), Python reinforces a programming style that uses fundamental limits and factors without participating in class definitions.

Regardless, for JavaScript, there is always a need for class participation.

Python, on the other hand, supports making much higher ventures and better code reuse through a genuine article orchestrated programming style, where classes and heritage expect a critical activity.

Python versus Perl

Python and Perl start from a near establishment (Unix scripting, which both have long outgrown), and sport various equivalent features, anyway, have a substitute perspective.

Perl stresses support for typical application- assignments; for example, by having worked in common explanations, investigating records, and report creating features.

Python underlines support for essential programming strategies; for instance, data structure plan and organized programming, and urges programming architects to create understandable (and along these lines reasonable) code by giving a rich anyway not unreasonably cloud documentation.

Subsequently, Python approaches Perl yet on occasion beats it in its one of a kind application territory; in any case, Python has a genuine nature well past Perl's claim to fame.

Python versus Tcl

Tcl likewise to Python is used as an application development language, similarly as a free programming language.

In any case, Tcl, which for the most part, stores all data as strings, is frail on data structures, and executes conventional code significantly more delayed than Python.

Tcl in like manner needs features required for creating vast activities, for instance, estimated namespaces.

Along these lines, while a "regular" immense application using Tcl, as a rule, contains Tcl enlargements written in C or C++ that are express to that application, a related Python application can much of the time be written in "Complete Python Code."

Tcl is one of the redeeming qualities is the Tk tool compartments, whereas Python has gotten an interface to Tk as its standard GUI portion library.

Python versus Smalltalk

Possibly the best differentiation among Python and Smalltalk is Python's progressively "standard" language structure, which allows software experts ease in working.

Like Smalltalk, Python has dynamic forming, which is increasing the usage and functionalities of this programming language.

Nevertheless, Python perceives worked in object types of data from customer described classes.

However, Smalltalk's standard library data types are dynamically refined.

Python's library has more workplaces for overseeing Internet and WWW substances, for instance, email, HTML, and FTP.

Python can store both standard modules and customer modules in individual records, which can be improved or coursed outside the framework.

There is more than one decision for affixing a Graphical User Interface (GUI) to a Python program, whereas Smalltalk lacks this attribute.

Python versus C++

Python and C++ are the programming languages used for the development of high-level projects.

Both Python and C++ languages vary from one another from numerous points of view.

C++ is begun from C language with various ideal models and gives multiple in-built components for creating programs, whereas Python is similar to the English language with highly simple syntax.

Python is universally useful and one of the high-level programming languages.

A variable can be utilized straightforwardly without its presentation while composing code in Python.

In C++, a separate program needs to get ordered on each working framework on which the code is to be executed, while Python has frameworks that allow users to run a program in small sections

Python gives the capacity to compose, and run on any platform' that empowers it to keep running on all the working frameworks.

C++ is inclined to memory spill as it doesn't give separate execution options and uses pointers to a vast degree.

Python has inbuilt trash accumulation and dynamic memory portion process that empower proficient use of memory.

C++, nowadays, is commonly utilized for planning equipment.

It is first portrayed in C++ pursued by its examination, structurally compelled, and wanted to build up a register-move level equipment depiction language.

 Python is utilized as a scripting language, and now it is also used for a non-scripting reason.

Likewise, Python has an independent executable application with the assistance of some built-in functions.

Python versus Common Lisp and Scheme

Common Lisp and Scheme are close to Python in their dynamic semantics.

Python has logical limits like those of Lisp.

Their programs can have unlimited consistent conditions to perform a particular task of extended length.

Common Lisp and Scheme have some complex variations in their coding schemes only understandable by programmers.

In contrast, Python has simple, easy to understand, and straightforward coding to manage every line of code.

Python vs. Golang

Golang is quite an adaptable language, just like Python.

Both languages do not require excessive instructional exercise and are easy to understand and executable.

Golang is also called the Go language, and Google developed it in 2009.

Python underpins numerous programming ideal models and has a vast standard library; ideal models included are object-oriented, basic, practical, and procedural.

Go underpins multi-worldview like procedural, practical, and simultaneous.

Its sentence structure is customarily originating from C; however, it has a smooth syntax structure, which requires less effort.

It is observed that Python and 'Go' have too many differences.

Take, for example, Golang doesn't use the feature of *try-except,* rather it allows functions to show problems together with a conclusion.

Therefore, before using a function, it is required to check that error will not return.

Python is mostly utilized in web applications, whereas Golang prime focus is to become a system language.

However, Go is also utilized in some web applications. Python has no memory management, but Golang provides efficient memory management.

Python does not have a concurrency mechanism, whereas Golang, on the other hand, has a built-in concurrency mechanism.

In terms of safety, Python is a strongly typed language that is compiled, so it adds an extra layer of security whereas Go is not too bad since each factor must have a sort related to it.

It implies a designer can't let away the subtleties, which will further prompt bugs.

Python has a greater number of libraries than Golang.

Python is more concise than Golang.

Python is the best option for basic programming, as it gets difficult to write complicated functions with it.

However, Golang is much better in complex programming than Python

Not only this but also one significant dissimilarity exists.

Python is a language that can be typed dynamically, whereas Go is not dynamic.

The main reason behind this fact is that Python developers can easily understand Golang without any problem.

- Python focuses on simple and clear syntax, and spotless grammar of Go drives correctly to high clarity.
- The static composting of Go lines up with the standard of "express is superior to understood" in Python.

So it can be said that Python is the best option for software engineers and developers all around the globe.

But because Python is a dynamically typed language, its performance is lesser than Golang due to its uniqueness of statically typed.

Therefore, it is better to use both languages simultaneously.

For coding, give priority to Golang and use Python otherwise.

Python versus Node.js

It's critical to recollect that Node.js isn't a programming language like Python, yet instead a runtime domain for JavaScript.

Hence, writing in Node.js means you're utilizing a similar language on the frontend and the backend.

Favorable Circumstances of Python over Node.js

At a further advanced level, JavaScript can be hard to comprehend for developers with less Node.js experience.

They may commit some genuinely basic errors, hindering progress simultaneously.

It isn't the situation with Python since it's simpler to use for less experienced developers.

The slip-ups made by them will have, to a lesser extent, a negative effect on improvement.

Lower Section Point

Frameworks, for example, Django is supportive, increment the nature of your code, and accelerate the way toward composing.

More Applications

Node.js is, for the most part, utilized for the web, while the uses of Python are far more noteworthy.

The all-inclusiveness and flexibility of Python are among the top reasons why the language is an excellent fit for slanting advancements, for example, data science.

Better Usage

JavaScript runtime conditions and frameworks all unexpectedly actualize the language; Node.js is no exemption.

In all honesty, the ecosystem of JavaScript is somewhat of a wreck—however, not even close to as terrible as it used to be.

Python doesn't have that issue, which is the reason it's more straightforward and simpler to utilize.

It additionally makes the language quicker to write in, although Node.js is not slow.

It's crucial to know JavaScript if you wish to utilize Node.js since you're managing a similar language on the frontend and the backend.

Less Obstinate Ecosystem

Node.js has unique features that pushes developers through indicators about "what they need to use and when they need to use" when they are working through this programming language.

It has a lot of built-in packages that developers need to understand.

That's why, with the improvement of programming libraries, the developers will have to develop their skills to that level.

Coding Everything in JavaScript

The JavaScript is used for frontend and backend programming with the assistance of Node.js to achieve the best results.

It saves a lot of time and makes the work easy for users. Nowadays, IT experts use this language as much as possible to perform web-based programming tasks.

Quick Development and a Huge Network

Since 2012, Python has been reliably lauded for its incredible network and support—and which is all well and good.

With its large number of libraries and frameworks, it has quick development procedures by calling the required library or function.

Nowadays, JavaScript is similarly also upheld.

It continues developing without any indications of halting and stays particularly ahead of the pack of the most powerfully growing languages in the business.

Advancement History of Python and JavaScript

JavaScript has seen a lot of developing agonies.

Its code was rejected many times when it was created, and its old adaptations are as yet making similar issues today.

Overall, Python has the high ground here.

The documentation and inclusion of Python are both better than Node.js.

With regard to unwavering quality, Python has consistently been in front of JavaScript.

Inclining Advances

The tumultuous ecosystem of JavaScript additionally makes Node.js excessively precarious and erratic to depend on for drifting innovations.

As a result of the critical issues of JavaScript patterns, JavaScript innovations become obsolete significantly more rapidly.

It is the reason Node.js is an unsafe decision for rising innovative trends.

Python doesn't represent that hazard since it presents significant changes gradually.

The language is an ideal fit for slanting innovations, for example, machine learning or data science, with its first-class specialists and library support.

Execution and Speed

Node.js may battle with executing many assignments immediately.

The code isn't composed well overall; your program will perform ineffectively and work gradually.

It may occur with Python, but Python frameworks, for example, Django, provide instant support to assist your program to run smoothly.

It's one more case of Python making life easier for developers.

Your program quality is everything—it's the main factor to think about when choosing the programming language for your final product shape.

Python works better for certain undertakings, and Node.js works better for other people.

Your decision ought to depend completely on whether you have great Python or JavaScript developers in your group.

This contention is invalid on the off chance that you happen to have full-stack developers with the two programming languages;

nonetheless, those are difficult to find, so you need to decide your programming strategy before you start.

Python versus PHP

From the improvement perspective, PHP is a web-situated language.

A PHP application is increasingly similar to a lot of exclusive content, possibly with a separate semantic section point.

Python is an adaptable language that can be additionally applied for web improvement.

A web application dependent on Python is an undeniable application stacked into memory with its inside state, spared from the inquiry to the solicitation.

When choosing between Python or PHP for web applications, focus on the following qualities:

Python versus PHP for Web Improvement Correlation

Patterns and prevalence of a programming language are critical these days.

A few clients and program proprietors need to utilize the most famous and advertised advancements for their undertakings.

As PHP has command over web-application programming and is widely used among the developer's community, it is considered the best option to achieve high-speed applications.

Whereas Python also works for web-applications, the main agenda of this programming language is Data Science.

Frameworks

Python has a lot of functional libraries that are famous across the world, for example, Pandas, Numpy, and more.

Similarly, there are highly efficient open-source code mechanisms.

PHP has a different approach towards code quality and a system of innovative addition in this programming source.

There are popular frameworks in Python, but the most useful are Django and Flask.

Globally, developers are using these frameworks to enhance the speed of their work.

PHP language doesn't use frameworks. Instead, it focuses on calling libraries built by other PHP communities.

It is an established reality that Python's framework will change soon because of the developing network of Python.

Chapter 9: Data Cleaning and Preparation

The next topic that we need to take a look at in our process of data science is known as data cleaning and preparation.

During the course of doing our own data analysis and modeling, a lot of time is going to be spent on preparing the data before it even enters into the model that we want to use.

The process of data preparation is going to include a lot of different tasks, including loading, cleaning, transforming, and rearranging the data.

These tasks are so important and take up so much of our time; it is likely that an analyst is going to spend at least 80 percent of their time on this.

Sometimes the way that we see the data stored in a database or a file is not going to provide us with the right format when we work with a particular task.

Many researchers find that it is easier to do ad hoc processing of the data, taking it from one form to another, working with some programming language.

The most common programming languages to use to make this happen include Perl, R, Python, or Java.

The good news here though is that the Pandas library that we talked about before, along with the features it gets from Python, can provide us with everything that we need.

It has the right tools that are fast, flexible, and high-level that will enable us to get the data manipulated into the form that is most needed at that time.

There are a few steps that we are able to work with in order to clean the data and get it all prepared, and these include:

What Is Data Preparation?

Let's suppose that you are going through some of the log files of a website and analyzing these, hoping to find out which IP out of all the options the spammers are coming from.

Or you can use this to figure out which demographic on the website is leading to more sales.

An analysis has to be performed on the data with two important columns to provide answers to such questions and more.

These are going to include the number of hits that have been made to the website, and the IP address of the hit.

As we can imagine here, the log files that you are analyzing are not going to be structured, and they could contain a lot of textual information that is unstructured.

To keep this simple, preparing the log file to extract the data in the format that you require in order to analyze it can be the process known as data preparation.

Data preparation is a big part of the whole data science process.

According to CrowdFlower, which is a provider of data enrichment platforms that data scientists can work with, it is seen that out of 80 data scientists, they will spend their day in the following:

- 60 percent of their time is spent on organizing and then cleaning the data they have collected.
- 19 percent is spent on collecting the sets of data that they want to use.
- 9 percent is used to mine the data that they have collected and prepared in order to draw the necessary patterns.
- 3 percent of their time will be spent doing any of the necessary training for the sets of data.
- 4 percent of the time is going to be spent trying to refine the algorithms that were created and working on getting them better at their jobs.

- 5 percent of the time is spent on some of the other tasks that are needed for this job.

As we can see from the statistics of the survey above, it helps us to see that most of the time for that data scientist is spent in preparing the data, which means they have to spend a good deal of time organizing, cleaning, and collecting, before they are even able to start on the process of analyzing the data.

There are a few valuable tasks of data science like data visualization and data exploration, but the least enjoyable process of data science is going to be the data preparation.

The amount of time that you actually will spend on preparing the data for a specific problem with the analysis is going to depend directly on the health of the data.

If there are a lot of errors, missing parts, and duplicate values, then this is a process that will take a lot longer.

But if the data is well-organized and doesn't need a lot of fixing, then the data preparation process is not going to take that long at all.

Why Do I Need Data Preparation?

One question that a lot of people have when it is time to work on the process of data preparation is why they need to do it in the first place.

It may seem to someone who is just getting started in this field that collecting the data and getting it all as organized as possible would be the best steps to take, and then they can go on to making their own model.

But there are a few different reasons why data preparation will be so important to this process, and they will include the following:

- The set of data that you are working with could contain a few discrepancies in the codes or the names that you are using.

- The set of data that you are working with could contain a lot of outliers or some errors that mess with the results.

- The set of data that you are working with will lack your attributes of interest to help with the analysis.

- The set of data that you want to explore is not going to be qualitative, but it is going to be quantitative.

    These are not the same things, and often having more quality is going to be the most important.

Each of these things has the potential to really mess up the model that you are working on and could get you results or predictions that are not as accurate as you would like.

Taking the time to prepare your data and get it clean and ready to go can solve this issue and will ensure that your data is going to be more than ready to use in no time.

What Are the Steps for Data Preparation?

At this point, we need to take some time to look at some of the steps that are needed to handle the data preparation for data mining.

The first step is to clean the data.

This is one of the first and most important steps to handling the data and getting it prepared.

We need to go through and correct any of the data that is inconsistent by filling out some of the values that are missing and then smoothing out the outliers and any data that is making a lot of noise and influencing the analysis in a negative manner.

There is the possibility that we end up with many rows in our set of data that do not have a value for the attributes of interest, or they could be inconsistent data that is there as well.

In some cases, there are records that have been duplicated or some other random error that shows up.

We need to tackle all of these issues with the data quality as quickly as possible in order to get a model at the end that provides us with an honest and reliable prediction.

There are a few methods that we can use to handle some of the missing values.

The method that is chosen is going to be dependent on the requirement either by ignoring the tuple or filling in some of the missing values with the mean value of the attribute.

This can be done with the help of the global constant or with some of the other Python machine learning techniques, including the Bayesian formulae or a decision tree.

We can also take some time to tackle the noisy data when needed.

It is possible to handle this in a manual manner.

Or there are several techniques of clustering or regression that can help us to handle this as well. You have to choose the one that is needed based on the data that you have.

The second step that we need to focus on here is going to be known as data integration.

This step is going to involve a few things like integrating the schema, resolving some of the conflicts of the data if any shows up, and even handling any of the redundancies that show up in the data that you are using.

Next on the list is going to be the idea of data transformation.

This step is going to be important because it will take time to handle some of the noise that is found in your data.

This step is going to help us to take out that noise from the data so it will not cause the analysis you have to go wrong.

We can also see the steps of normalization, aggregation, and generalization showing up in this step as well.

We can then move on to the fourth step, which is going to be all about reducing the data.

The data warehouse that you are using might be able to contain petabytes of data, and running an analysis on this complete set of data could take up a lot of time and may not be necessary for the goals that you want to get in the end with your model.

In this step, it is the responsibility of the data science to obtain a reduced representation of their set of data.

We want this set to be smaller in size than some of the others, but inclusive enough that it will provide us with some of the same analysis outcomes that we want.

This can be hard when we have a very large set of data, but there are a few reduction strategies for the data that we can apply.

Some of these are going to include numerosity reduction, aggregation, data cube, and dimensionality reduction, and more, based on the requirements that you have.

And finally, the fifth step of this is going to be known as data discretization.

The set of data that you are working with will contain three types of attributes.

These three attributes are going to include continuous, nominal, and ordinal.

Some of the algorithms that you will choose to work with only handle the attributes that are categorical.

This step of data discretization can help someone in data science divide continuous attributes into intervals, and can also help reduce the size of the data.

This helps us to prepare it for analysis.

Take your time with this one to make sure that it all matches up and does some of the things that you are expecting.

Many of the methods and the techniques that you are able to use with this part of the process are going to be strong and can get a lot of the work with you.

But even with all of these tools, it is still considered an area of research, one that many scientists are going to explore more and hopefully come up with some new strategies and techniques that you can use to get it done.

Handling the Missing Data

It is common for data to become missing in many applications of data analysis.

One of the goals of working with the Pandas library here is that we want to make it work with some of this missing data as easy and as painless as possible.

For example, all of the descriptive statistics that happen on the objects of Pandas exclude the missing data by default.

The way that this data is going to be represented in Pandas is going to have some problems, but it can be really useful for many of the users who decide to go with this kind of library.

For some of the numeric data that we may have to work with, the Pandas library is going to work with a floating-point value that is known as NaN, or not a number, to represent the data that is missing inside of our set of data.

In the Pandas library, we have adopted a convention that is used in the programming language of R in order to refer to the missing data.

This missing data is going to show up as NA, which means not available right now.

In the applications of statistics, NA data can either be data that doesn't exist at all, or that exists, but we are not going to be able to observe through problems in the collection of data.

When cleaning up the data to be analyzed, it is often important to do some of the analysis on the missing data itself to help identify the collection of the data and any problems or potential biases in the data that has been caused by the missing data.

There are also times when the data is going to have duplicates.

When you get information online or from other sets of data, it is possible that some of the results will be duplicated.

If this happens often, then there is going to be a mess with the insights and predictions that you get.

The data is going to lean towards the duplicates, and it will not work the way that you would like.

There are ways that you can work with the Pandas library in order to really improve this and make sure that the duplicates are eliminated or are limited at least a little bit.

There is so much that we are able to do when it comes to working with data preparation in order to complete the process of data mining and getting the results that we want in no time with our analysis.

Make sure to take some time on this part, as it can really make or break the system that we are trying to create.

If you do spend enough time on it, and ensure that the data is as organized and clean as possible, you are going to be happy with the results and ready to take on the rest of the process.

Chapter 10: Data Visualization

Data visualization is an important element for every data scientist.

During the early periods of a project, you will need to perform an exploratory data analysis to identify insights into your data.

Creating visualizations allows you to simplify things, particularly with a wide-dimensional dataset.

Towards the end of your project, you need to deliver the final result in a transparent and compelling manner that your audience can understand.

Data Visualization to the End-User

Usually, the data scientist has a role in submitting their insights to the final user.

The results can be conveyed in different ways:

- *A single presentation.* In **the** following case, the research questions consist of one-shot deals because the business decision extracted from them will direct the organization to a given course for several years to come.

    For instance, company investment decisions.

- *Do you distribute the goods from two distribution centers or just one?*

  Where are they supposed to be located for the best efficiency?

  When the decision is made, the exercise might not be repeated until you retire.

  In the following case, the results are generated as a report with a presentation as the icing on the cake.

- *A new viewport on data.* The most common example of this is customer segmentation.

For sure, the segments will be send using reports and presentations, but in essence, they comprise of tools, but not the final result itself.

Once a clear and important customer segmentation is identified, it can be supplied back to the database as a new channel on the data from which it was extracted.

From this point, people can create their own reports.

For instance, how many products were sold to every customer segment?

- *For a real-time, dashboard—your functions as a data scientist don't complete once you have the new information.*

You can send your information back to the database and get done with it.

However, when other people start to create reports on the discovered gold nugget, they can interpret it incorrectly and generate reports that don't make sense.

Since you are the data scientist that found this new information, you need to set the example.

In the following case, you need to create the first refreshable report so that the rest can learn from it and use your footsteps.

Creating the first dashboard is still a means to reduce the delivery time of your insights to the final user who wants to make use of it daily.

By doing this, they already have something to build upon until the reporting department discovers the time to establish a permanent report regarding the company's reporting software.

You may have discovered that some important elements are at play:

- *First, what type of decision are you supporting?*

  Is it strategic or operational?

  Strategic decisions need you to conduct an analysis and generate a report.

But still, operational decisions require the report to be updated often.

- *What is the size of your organization?*

    For smaller organizations, you will deal with the general cycle.

    This one ranges from collection to reporting.

    For bigger teams, reporters could be available to create the dashboards for you.

    Still, in the last part, creating a prototype dashboard can be relevant because it provides an example and reduces the delivery time.

Matplotlib is a great Python library that can be used to build your data visualizations.

However, designing the data, parameters, and plots can get messy and tiresome to do regularly.

This section will guide you through data visualizations and create some rapid and easy functions with the help of Python's Matplotlib.

You will learn how to create basic plots using Seaborn, Matplotlib, and Pandas visualization.

Python offers many graphing libraries that are packed with a lot of features.

No matter whether you want to describe an interactive, or complex Python plots, it delivers a powerful library.

To provide some overview, the popular plotting libraries consist of:

- **Seaborn.** This has an advanced interface and important default styles.

- **Plotly.** This is important in the development of significant plots.

- **Visualization using Pandas.** It is easy to apply interface and has been built on Matplotlib.

- **Ggplot.** This one relies on R's ggplot2 and applies the Grammar of Graphics.

Matplotlib

This is the most common Python library.

It is a low library type that has a Matlab interface that has more freedom.

Matplotlib is important for creating basic graphs such as bar charts, line charts, and histograms.

You can import the following library by using the following line of code:

```
import matplotlib.pyplot as plt
```

Line Chart

The Matplotlib library allows the development of a line chart by applying the plot method.

Still, it is possible to create multiple columns using a single graph by plotting and looping every column on the same axis.

Histogram

By using Matplotlib, you can design a histogram using the hist method.

In case you relay categorical data like column points, it will help determine the likelihood of each class happening.

Bar Chart

In case you want to show data in a bar chart, then the bar function is useful.

The bar chart is not automatically created using the frequency of a category, so you will require to use Pandas to achieve this.

The bar chart is useful for grouping data that doesn't spread categories because it can become messy.

Visualization Using Pandas

Pandas represent an advanced level of open-source libraries.

It is a simple library that represents data structures and data analysis tools.

Visualization, with the help of Pandas, makes it easy to create data frames and series.

Still, it has an advanced level of API than the Matplotlib.

As a result, the minimum code is required for similar results.

If you want to install Pandas, then you require to run the pip command.

The Objective of Visualization

Data communication and exploration are the major focus of data visualization.

Once data is visualized, the patterns become visible.

You will immediately tell whether there is an increasing trend or the relative magnitude of something in connection to other factors.

Rather than tell people the long list of numbers, why not display the numbers to them for better clarity?

For instance, let's consider the worldwide trend search on the word 'bitcoin.'

You should see that there is a temporary rise in the bitcoin interest, but it starts to decrease after the peak.

Overall, during the peak interval, there's a huge hype connected to the technological and social effects of bitcoin.

Again, the following hype decreases because people understand it, or it's a common thing related to hypes.

No matter the situation, data visualization helps us to determine the patterns in a very clear style.

Keep in mind the importance of data visualization is to explore data.

In the following case, you can quickly choose the patterns as well as the data send to us.

This is critical when you submit it to the public audience.

Others may decide to go for a quick brief of the data without rushing into detail.

You don't really need to disturb them with texts and numbers.

What presents a wide effect is the way you build them using numbers and texts.

What sets a big difference is how you define the data so that individuals can quickly recall its importance.

This is where data visualization becomes helpful to allow people to mine data and communicate whatever you are trying to speak.

There are numerous methods of visualizing data.

The Simplest Method to Complex Visualization of Data

Visualizations are a powerful skill that every data scientist needs to be aware of to create excellent data.

It is more than just creating beautiful charts, representing the dataset's information in a way that is easy for individuals to learn.

When you have the right visualization, an individual can quickly learn the patterns and information that is found beneath the data.

In the early stages of a project, you will conduct an exploratory data analysis to generate insights into your data. Creating visualizations will increase your analysis.

At the end of your project, it is vital to submit your final results in a brief and compelling manner such that any audience can be able to read.

There's no doubt your visualizations to the next stage will let you defeat your next presentation.

This section will explore ways in which you can define an attractive, complex data visualization.

You will apply the Plotly python library that is excellent in creating interactive visualizations.

Overview of Plotly

Plotly represents an interactive, browser-depended graphic Python library.

It is a library that allows you to improve the visualization capabilities compared to the standard Matplotlib.

There are two benefits of applying Plotly instead of other Python libraries such as Matplotlib, Pandas, and Seaborn. That is:

- The ease of application.

    This will define an interactive plot and other complex graphics.

    Performing the same operation using other libraries takes a lot of work.

- It provides additional functionalities.

Since Plotly is designed from D3.js, the plotting capability is more powerful than other plotting libraries.

The Sunburst charts and many more are possible using Plotly.

Building Attractive Plots Using Plotly

Plotly is useful in building fancy plots.

To start, first, let's import Plotly and its internal graph objects component.

You will also import Pandas to load the dataset.

```
import plotly
import plotly.graph_objs as go
import Pandas as pd
```

To read the dataset, you basically write a one-liner in Pandas.

Scatter Plots

For this particular section, we are going to plot a scatter plot for sales price against the year built.

To achieve that, you will need to define a scatter graph object and store it in a trace.

```python
trace = go.Scatter(
    x = data['YearBuilt'],
    y = data['SalePrice'],
    mode = 'markers',
    showlegend = True
)
plot_data = [trace]
```

Then, to plot, you only write a single line.

```python
plotly.offline.plot(plot_data, filename='basic-scatter')
```

The following command will create a new tab within your browser with the plot.

Graph interactivity comes automatically built-in with Plotly.

Box Plots

This time, we will look at the box plots.

The process is quite similar.

For that reason, we are going to define a graph object, store it into a trace, and then represent it in a browser.

```
import plotly
import plotly.graph_objs as go

import Pandas as pd

data = pd.read_csv('train.csv')

trace = go.Box(
  x = data['YearBuilt'],
  y = data['SalePrice'],
  marker = {'color': 'green'},
  showlegend = True,
)
plot_data = [trace]

plotly.offline.plot(plot_data, filename='basic-box')
```

The box plot will feature attractive properties with box plots.

By default, we attain the same zooming, panning, and point of selection.

Now that the box plot exists, if you hover around each box plot, it will reveal the following:

- Median
- 1st and 3rd quartiles
- Min and Max values of the data range
- The upper and/or lower fences if there are outliers

Heat Maps

Heat maps are a critical tool for data scientists.

They are effective for displaying the association between multiple feature variables in a single graph plus the relative significance of each relationship.

To demonstrate the way your Heat Maps can be improved with Plotly, we are going to create a correlation matrix of the House Prices dataset as a heat map.

```
import plotly
import plotly.graph_objs as go
import Pandas as pd
data = pd.read_csv('train.csv')
corrmat = data.corr()
trace = go.Heatmap(z=corrmat, x=corrmat.columns.tolist(), y=corrmat.columns.tolist())
plot_data = [trace]
plotly.offline.plot(plot_data, filename='basic-heatmap')
```

Heat maps in Matplotlib can be somehow difficult because you cannot identify the correct value of each cell—you can only tell from the color.

You can write the code to make it interactive, but that's probably the hassle in Matplotlib.

Plotly provides interactivity beyond the box, so when you plot a heat map, you get an attractive overview and an option to confirm exact values when needed.

Both the pan-and-zoom functionality of Plotly are super clean, providing an easy mean to perform a comprehensive exploration from a visual point of view.

These are just to indicate the significance and possibilities of applying Plotly.

Keep in mind that you can create a publication using quality data visualizations. Additionally, you can change the example codes to your objective.

There's no need to invent something unique.

You can copy the right sections and apply them to your data.

Probably, in the future, there will be easier and effective methods to build data visualizations, especially when dealing with huge datasets.

You can still build animated presentations that can change with time.

Whichever way, the main goal of data visualization is to communicate data.

You can select other methods, but the goal normally remains the same.

You have learned general aspects of data visualization.

You have learned that data visualization is the practice of understanding data by representing it in a graphical style so that trends may not be seen exposed.

Python provides many different graphic libraries that are packed with lots of different attributes.

Conclusion

It was a long journey, but it's certainly not the end.

Data science is a massive field of study that requires years of learning and practice before you can master it.

This shouldn't discourage you, however!

Embrace it as a challenge that you can undertake in order to broaden your horizons and improve your knowledge of all that is data science and machine learning.

This book offers you the fundamental knowledge you need to get started, but keep in mind that no book or even teacher can do everything for you.

You need to work hard by putting each building block in its place as you advance.

Data science is a highly complex topic that has continuously been developed for decades.

It is constantly evolving, and it can be challenging to keep up with all the past, present, and future concepts.

With that being said, this isn't supposed to discourage you from pursuing this field.

You don't necessarily need a computer science degree in order to learn all aspects of data science.

What you do need, however, is that spark that urges you to learn more and put everything new to the test by working with real data sets and actual data science projects.

Acquire more books and join online communities of data scientists, programmers, statisticians, and machine learning enthusiasts!

You can benefit a lot from working with others.

Expose yourself to other perspectives and ideas as soon as possible, even when you barely know the basics.

The learning process receives a boost when you have other people with similar goals helping you out.

Almost everyone will agree with the statement that big data has arrived in a big way and has taken the business world by storm.

But what is the future of data analysis, and will it grow?

What are the technologies that will grow around it?

What is the future of big data?

Will it grow more?

Or is the big data going to become a museum article soon?

What is cognitive technology?

What is the future of fast data?

The data volume will keep on growing.

There is practically no question in the minds of people that we'll keep on developing a larger and larger quantity of data, especially after taking into consideration the number of internet-connected devices and handheld devices is going to grow exponentially.

The ways we undertake data analysis will show marked improvement in the upcoming years.

Although SQL will remain the standard tool, we'll see other tools such as Spark emerging as a complementary method for the data analysis, and their number will keep on growing as per reports.

More and more tools will become available for data analysis, and some of them will not need the analyst.

Microsoft and Salesforce have announced some combined features which will allow the non-coders to create apps for viewing the business data.

The prescriptive analytics will get built into the business analytics software, and IDC predicts that 50 percent of all software related to business analysis will become available with all the business intelligence it needs by the year 2020.

In addition to these features, real-time streaming insight into the big data will turn into a hallmark for the data winners moving forward.

The users will be looking to use this data for making informed decisions within real-time by using programs such as Spark and Kafka.

The topmost strategic trend that will emerge is machine learning. Machine learning will become a mandatory element for big data preparation and predictive analysis in businesses going forward.

You can expect big data to face huge challenges as well, especially in the field of privacy of user details.

The new private regulations enforced by the European Union clearly intend to protect the personal information of the users.

Various companies will have to address privacy controls and processes.

It is predicted that most of the business ethics violations will be related to data in the upcoming years.

Soon you can pretty much expect all companies to have a chief data officer in place.

Forrester says that this officer will rise in significance within a short period of time, but certain kinds of businesses and generation gaps might decrease their significance in the upcoming future.

Autonomous agents will continue to play a significant role, and they will keep on being a huge trend as per Gartner.

These agents include autonomous vehicles, smart advisers, virtual personal assistants, and robots.

The staffing required for the data analysis will keep on expanding, and people from scientists to analysts to architects to the experts in the field of data management will be needed.

However, a crunch in the availability of big data talent might see the large companies develop new tactics.

Some large institutes predict that various organizations will use internal training to get their issues resolved.

A business model having big data in the form of service can be seen on the horizon.

Data science is a complex field that requires a lot of dedication from you due to the amount of information you need to absorb.

This book hands you the tools you need to study every concept and guides you with clear examples of code and data sets.

The rest is up to you!

You have the fundamentals below your belt, and now you can continue your journey to become a data scientist!